THE ARMED FORCES OFFICER

AMERICAN FORCES INFORMATION SERVICE

DEPARTMENT OF DEFENSE

The American Forces Information Service
does not stock copies of this publication for general
distribution. For additional copies, contact your command,
or your service publication distribution center

DoD GEN-36A*
DA Pam 600-2(Rev. 1988)*
NAVEDTRA 46905-A*
 Navy Stock No.
 0503-LP-001-1760
AFP 190-13(Rev. 1988)*
NAVMC 2563(Rev. 1988)*

*This publication supersedes DoD GEN-36/DA Pam 600-2/NAVEDTRA 46905/AFP
190-13/NAVMC 2563(Rev. 75), dated July 22, 1975.

Contents

Introduction

When the original, hard-cover edition of this work appeared in November 1950, it opened with a brief preface: "This manual for leadership has been prepared for use by the Department of the Army, the Department of the Navy and the Department of the Air Force, and is published for the information and guidance of all concerned."

The note was signed "G. C. Marshall." Gen. George C. Marshall was then serving as secretary of defense. Some years earlier, while serving as Army chief of staff, he had inspired the undertaking due to his personal conviction that all American military officers share common ethical and moral ground. Individual services were commanded by men of integrity, honor and great leadership. The newly created Department of Defense, however, was a harness that chafed at the historical autonomy of the services.

This version, while holding with the purpose outlined and adhering to the broad philosophical guidelines provided by the original author, Brig. Gen. S. L. A. Marshall, has been modified by the experience of the past 38 years. During that time, we have experienced triumph and disaster. The nation has moved from a naive optimism where anything is possible to a more mature reality where most things are possible, if we are willing to pay the price.

This book is based on the firm conviction that our nation is always at least on the threshold of greatness and is worth whatever it takes to maintain our ideals. It is about the love of duty and the knowledge that there is no higher calling than that of an Armed Forces officer. Old-fashioned concepts of service, of loyalty, of duty and of being better than you think is possible are included because they work and apply in a complex and volatile world that sometimes seems to lack a foundation for action.

Special Trust and Confidence

This book is about American Armed Forces officers of all services and grades. It is an American book and makes no apology for its point of view. The book's roots are in the writings of both military and civil leaders; it depends heavily on the thoughts and philosophical guidance of Army Brig. Gen. S. L. A. Marshall, who wrote the original and classic "Armed Forces Officer." It was written to provide a foundation of thought, conduct, standards and duty for officers.

It examines the qualities that have led to greatness. Even though the book uses examples of great leaders in American history, it is not about generals and admirals. It is about those special obligations, responsibilities, demands and standards that you and all military officers must maintain.

To begin with, all Armed Forces officers swear the same oath that every president and military officer has taken since George Washington became the first president of our nation and commander in chief of its armed forces. They have sworn or affirmed that they will uphold the Constitution of the United States against all enemies, foreign or domestic, to bear true faith and allegiance to the same and to discharge well and faithfully the duties of the office without any mental reservation or purpose of evasion.

An officer who swears or affirms that simple oath joins a 200-year tradition by making a commitment to our nation and our Constitution. It also is a warning to any potential enemy. Just as in times past, it is the commitment of "life, fortune and sacred honor." It is a guarantee to the nation and to any enemy of the nation that the officer is prepared to take any action necessary to keep our nation free.

The new officer is given a commission stating that the president of the United States has granted the officer authority, having reposed "special trust and confidence" in the "patriotism, valor, fidelity and abilities" of that officer.

A commission is never lightly given. It must be earned and deserved. It does not mean that the officer instantly becomes a leader. It means the officer has been found worthy to enter a profession that dedicates itself to the leadership of American fighting forces and the defense of the nation.

The uniform, devices and insignia all identify the officer with the power of the United States of America. As the officer serves honorably and grows in skill and knowledge, he or she will live a life of challenge, commitment, national service and dedication. While that may sound like the lifestyle of a Trappist monk in the 13th century, nothing could be farther from the truth and, at the same time, closer.

Top Gun, a popular movie during the mid-1980s, looks at both sides of this axiom. The hero is a professional flyer whose skills, dedication and eventual selflessness lead to combat success against the enemy. Along the way to this dedicated professionalism, his recklessness and inability to "follow the rules" cost him his best friend and partner in flight. Only his ability to learn self-discipline and to put the needs of the nation before his own lead to his eventual success. While the movie portrays one major requirement of the Armed Forces officer, it also manages to portray a facet of military life that is all too often overlooked. For most military officers, the lifestyle is composed of dedication, personal growth, family and, a cornerstone of any existence, fun. Some will argue that the concept of fun has no place in the portrayal of the Armed Forces officer. Without fun or a pleasurable existence, however, it would be difficult to retain any officer past the initial obligation.

Fun is not the goal. But fun times and enjoyment of the job and the total environment make the balanced lifestyle attractive and meaningful. And it is a balanced style of life. The military lifestyle offers more opportunities for personal growth, family growth, education and a hundred other things than can be found in any other profession.

Too strong a statement? Not at all! From the cleric to the engineer-from the policeman to the philosopher-from the undertaker to the band leader-all have a place in military life and can, to use a potent Army recruiting slogan, "be all you can be." Look at any military base. There are places to train, educate, party, babysit, meditate and grow. The limits on this growth are the limits of the individual officer.

A young officer in Harvard Medical School put it this way: "For me, the military is the ideal lifestyle. I get paid every month, get to attend the best schools in the world and can always take the time to get better at my job. In return, I have to be willing to put my life on the line. Seems like a simple trade for me! I can't lose."

As an officer lives up to the demands of the profession, the nation will honor the service as it does no other profession. Of course, there are periods of national disenchantment. There are times when the fact of service requires additional identification to cash a check or to buy a house. This, however, is not the result of national rejection of the military.

The My Lai tragedy was not so much that troops snapped under the pressures of combat and murdered civilians. Such an unacceptable act, sadly, has the potential for happening in any military unit under stresses of combat. Rather, the lack of understanding and the outrage of the nation focused on the simple fact that it was an American officer who failed to stop the troops. "Where was his morality?" "Where was his courage?" And, most importantly, "Why didn't he stop what he knew to be wrong?"

There are neither easy answers nor acceptable excuses. There is only the fact that the officer in charge failed to live up to the national Expectation of what an officer must be. As a result, he was convicted of a military offense.

This obviously extreme example of the moral standards the nation demands of its officer corps emphasizes the moral imperative for personal honor in all officers. The assumption that American officers will maintain the highest standards makes it unnecessary for the American oath of office to include, as does the Russian oath, penalties for breaking the oath.

The military officer obviously is not the sole repository of national honor and national morality. Many Americans, in just as many professions, have codes of behavior and professional standards. The nation expects more from the military officer: It expects a living portrayal of the highest standards of moral and ethical behavior. The expectation is neither fair nor unfair; it is a simple fact of the profession. The future of the services and the well-being of its people depend on the public perception and fact of the honor, virtue and trustworthiness of the officer corps.

What may appear as unfair is that any breakdown of trust or in behavior by any single officer reflects on all. It makes no difference that the failure could be as simple as slovenly dress or as extreme as the loss of control of combat forces. Any scandal involving any officer affects the public perception of all officers. In the final analysis, the Armed Forces work for, and are responsible to, the public. If the American people cannot depend on an officer to live up to the standards of the profession, how can they entrust the officer with the lives of their sons and daughters?

The nation must be shown by daily example that the authority vested in the officer is well-placed and warranted. When the pendulum swings from favoritism to near rejection of the military due to national experiences that stir dissent, protest or anti-military clamor-and it will-the only choice for the military officer corps is a visible rededication to the precepts of honor, integrity and trust.

It will never be easy. Our complex world becomes even more so daily.

Today's officers Will face decisions and issues that were unthinkable just
A few years ago. The complex and difficult problems have no easy
solutions. There is no magic computer to provide precisely the right
answer. Approaching the profession with a firm understanding of honor,
integrity and duty makes the search simpler and the answer clearer.

Some Americans occasionally question the need for such high standards of conduct. After all, the concept of military officers is based on
the notion of "gentlemen," who, by definition, possess the ideal qualities
for military leadership. Many Western societies have operated
governments and armed forces on the assumption that the accident of
birth presupposed the ability to lead nations and armies. Landed or
monied status somehow gave one loyalty, courage, devotion to duty and
the ability to command. The practice of buying commissions was
designed to perpetuate this notion.

Only "gentlemen" could afford to purchase a commission, so only
gentlemen were officers. Occasional battle catastrophes resulted from
inept leadership, but so long as there was a preponderance of arms and
discipline, it was not impossible for the most inept officer to defeat na-
tive forces.

America quickly discarded the flawed system of selling commissions.
Allowing troops to elect officers worked only marginally better. We rapidly began to define leadership in terms of inherent qualities and teach-
able skills, based on the person rather than on the accident of birth.
The concept reflects the Constitution's notion of individual dignity and
value. Respect for individual rights is also the reason we have a long
history of disapproving of any action that demeans any member of our
military.

No military system can work unless the officer corps embodies high
standards of honor, integrity and subordination of self to national direction. Adherence to standards, as former Secretary of State Dean Rusk
stated, "makes it clearly impossible to conceive of a military assumption
of political power."

Asked to name the one quality that marks the outstanding officer,
Navy Vice Adm. William Ramsey, vice commander in chief of the U.S.
Space Command, replied without hesitation: "Integrity! Without integ-
rity, there is nothing." Lt. Gen. Winfield Scott, superintendent of the
U.S. Air Force Academy, answered similarly: "An officer's entire worth
lies in his personal integrity."

2

What Is an Officer?

You must know that it is no easy thing for a principle to become a man's own,
unless each day he maintain it and hear it maintained, as well as work it out in life.
                                                          -Epictetus

What does it take to make a good officer? What combination of
factors makes you different? Where do you draw the line? What do the
Armed Forces expect from you?

Junior officers who responded to those questions, as part of the revision of this book, showed a desire for specific direction and simple
answers to difficult and complex problems.

Good officers are competent at the profession, demonstrate by example
the highest standards of moral and ethical behavior and continue to try
to become better. Good officers spend a significant amount of time and
effort learning about their craft, themselves and the people who work
with them. They are surprised by the vagaries of fate but not by the
facts that exist. They understand both the failings and the possible
magnificence of human beings. They care deeply about nation, service and
duty. They are self-disciplined and self-motivating.

When David Glasgow Farragut became a midshipman at age 9, long
before the U.S. Naval Academy was established, it was a much simpler
world. When the superintendent at West Point made it a practice to take
the incoming class for nature walks along the Hudson River, it was still
an understandable world. When Dwight David Eisenhower, with sheer
skill and force of personality, was able to bring all of the viewpoints,
biases and national goals of many nations into a single international
fighting machine, it was still possible to be expert in many of the forces
that molded human destiny.

Sometime in the 1960s, perhaps as a result of the self-examination
process that came with the war in Vietnam, an old idea resurfaced among
some politicians and intellectuals: Peace is all-important and should be
obtained at any cost. The same idea has contributed to the collapse of

nations throughout history. (Carthagenians, for example, learned its price centuries ago.)

Peace-at-any-price thinking led to the perception that the United States, by resisting aggression, was the moral equivalent of the Soviet Union, if not an outright force for evil in the world. The belief implied that something is wrong with the notion that Western liberty is special, superior and worth defending. This phenomenon found adherents, took root and grew in the minds of many. The simple belief seemed to make some kind of sense at first glance. It made no sense to anyone who had a minimum of ethical education or had to do the fighting.

The most important thing worth noting as a response to concepts of moral equivalency and the conduct of combat is that Armed Forces officers continued to do their duty during the unpopular war in Vietnam, despite critics, street protests and political disputes back home.

The structure by which differing political systems come to agreements and accommodations is a diplomatic one. A major duty of the Armed Forces is to ensure that diplomatic initiatives get a reasonable hearing. To accomplish this requires an officer corps of exceptional dedication, responsibility and ethical behavior.

An Armed Forces officer is involved with the nation, service, unit, community, family and religion. The Armed Forces have always recognized the importance of religion to the lives of service members and been able to accommodate it. The individual officer must recognize that unit members may profess a wide range of faiths or no religion.

An Armed Forces officer does the homework necessary to be a complete and useful leader among the nation's warriors. The study never ends. It entails hard work and hard thinking about what the officer is, where his or her duty lies and what the person is trying to become. Taking the oath to support and defend the Constitution implies a requirement to know the Constitution. An officer preparing to defend against a specific enemy must know something about that enemy. The Armed Forces recognize that the continual learning process takes time and some guidance. The professional military education system, as good as it is, is just the basis for continual study and learning.

The Armed Forces officer always is physically ready to meet the job's challenges. Not everyone can win gold medals at the Olympic Games, but everyone can maintain the required physical capability. Excellent physical conditioning is related directly to the mental stamina (hat is a large part of leadership. Service academies recognize the importance of physical fitness in their motto that while not every athlete can be a cadet (or midshipman), every cadet (or midshipman) is of necessity an athlete.

Navy Vice Adm. James Stockdale has put much of the job of any military member in perspective. A longtime prisoner of war, he learned some of the lessons in the most brutal of schools. He learned them so well and taught them so well that he wears the nation's highest award, the Medal of Honor. His view is simple and direct, and it works: "If you don't lose your integrity, you can't be had and you can't be hurt. If you don't take the first shortcut or make the first compromise, that is, look for the tacit deal, you can't be had."

When counting beans, the answers are simple. In matters such as morals or ethics, specific answers are difficult to find.

Today's world is far more complex and more difficult to understand than the previous generation could ever imagine. Earlier officers could not foresee concepts like the German raiders, who drifted for months waiting for targets, or the British fleet steaming at 8 knots from Britain to the Falklands with the Russians-via a reconnaissance satellite-watching their progress and passing the information to the enemy. Affairs of men and nations are marvelously complex and only rarely are what they appear to be on the surface.

Consider a few basics:

* most people like predictability;
* most people do not want to make the effort to be different;
* most folks do not understand how good they really are.

A young officer, called upon to brief the commander of a major command, made an exceptional presentation. He spoke about one of the more technical areas of the training process, that of learning stations and the design of the stations. When he finished, he stepped to the left of the lectern and waited for comments. They were immediate and to the point. The general told the lieutenant, "I appreciate your remarks, but I do not think that you are correct. What I want is something totally different. And that is what we are going to have!"

The young officer thought for a moment and, to the surprise of the staff, responded:

"Sir, you are totally wrong! What you have told us to do will set training back some 30 years!"

The general, understandably hostile, asked, "Lieutenant, do you have any idea whom you are addressing?"

The young officer looked around the room for help, saw none, but took a chance. He answered:

"Sir, I am the nation's expert in learning stations. I wrote the book that your people use to design them. I have a doctorate in the field, and most people defer to my judgment. In short, sir, I am the best that you can get, and you, sir, are but the general who will make use of my knowledge."

Was he out of line? Of course he was. One reason some Armed Forces officers make flag rank, however, is their ability to recognize and develop their people's talents. This general ignored the all-too-obvious cheap shot and, with great tact and patience, gave the lieutenant and the entire staff a lesson. He easily could have chastised the young officer, humiliating him to the point where the officer would quit at the first opportunity. Instead, he taught the entire staff the necessity for acting on what an

7

officer knows to be correct; he taught a whole lot more about the ways to present that opinion.

He told the lieutenant to be seated and spoke to everyone in the room. "What that young man said is correct. If he is the nation's expert, then his judgment in that specific area represents the best input that I can get. I have to commend him for the courage to tell me the truth as he sees it. I don't like the way that he said it, but even in the way that he said it, he is right. I am the general, and I have to make the decisions. If all that I have to make that decision with is 'gut feel,' then that is what I'll use. But if I can get all members of the staff to give me both honest and reasonably polite responses to the issues at hand, then all of our jobs will be easier and the entire command will function better. Everyone, including the general, can, at times, be wrong. You are not serving any of us well if you permit that error to continue."

Later, the general had his aide give the young officer a copy of How to Win Friends and Influence People.

Armed Forces officers bring to mind the lines in Kipling's poem, "If-." They must keep their heads when all about them are losing theirs. When in combat, they must always remember that it is combat and not a maneuver taking place in a friendly land. There is no excuse for losing people or equipment because, "That's the way we do it at Station X in the States." There are good reasons to learn the lessons of the past and apply them to the current situation.

Exposed aircraft neatly lined on the tarmac, capital ships gathered in exposed harbors, the refusal to accept collect phone calls from crisis areas and the housing of troops in vulnerable facilities are examples of the lack of officer understanding of the threat of combat or terrorist attack.

Many more examples could be found. All are based on someone's notion of economics, expediency or promotion. All have resulted in the needless death of good people. All are unforgivable.

Responsibility and Privilege

RHIP-Rank hath its privileges. True or false? The answer is both.
As responsibility increases, it is both normal and commonplace that the
system provides for eliminating trifling, time-consuming annoyances. If
an Eisenhower is commanding an Allied invasion of Europe, it is not
unreasonable for him to have someone to plan, prepare and serve meals
or to get a uniform clean and ready to wear. An officer should never forget that privileges to senior officers free their hands for their primary
duties. There is, of course, another side of the matter. When people are
successful, they usually expect and appreciate the good things in life.

Retired Air Force Gen. Orvil A. Anderson started in the military by
digging ditches. He noticed one day, while digging in the rain and wind,
that there were few officers in the ditch with him and no aviation
officers in sight. That was adequate incentive for him. Re got out of the
ditch and into Officer Candidate School. He went to flight school and
wound up commanding the Air War College. Was privilege his primary
motivation? No! It was getting out of the ditch and drying off.

Except for proponents of the Japanese Theory Z style of leadership,
most sectors of society provide some set of perquisites, or "perks," to
reward increased responsibility. It could be as simple as the Marines'
practice at one hot, southwestern base where officers always get ice in
the snack bar drinks, or it could be a full staff of servants, cooks and
drivers. Ours is a capitalistic society, and most of our society accepts
the concept of reward. It does not accept unwarranted assumption of
privilege. Bill Mauldin's World War II cartoon illustrates what privilege
isn't. In the cartoon are two officers looking out over a beautiful
valley. One says to the other, "Nice view. Is there one for the enlisted
men?"

One of the keenest minds of our time said that responsibility is what
devolves upon a person, and privilege is what he ought not to take but
does. In a perfect universe, this would be true. Unfortunately, few of
us have found that universe. Instead, we must live and work in the one we
have. At all levels, people will aspire more and their ambition will be

firmer if getting ahead will mean for them an increase in the visible tokens of deference from the majority, rather than a simple boost in paycheck.

Abuse of privilege creates much of the friction between people. The root of the problem is not that privileges exist, but that they are exercised too often by people who are motivated not by duty, but by privilege. The officer who is most concerned with the responsibility of the profession will find little resentment of the exercise of the rightful privilege.

Americans get their backs up whenever they think they are being pushed around simply for the sake of the pushing. We understand and accept that privilege attends rank and station and that it is confirmed and modified by time and environment. What was right yesterday may be all wrong tomorrow, and what is proper in one set of circumstances may be wholly wrong in another.

Abuse of privilege by American officers was a concern during debates on the ratification of the Constitution. Mercy Warren, a prolific writer of the times, wrote that "ordinary citizens were dissatisfied with the high pretensions of the officers of the army, whose equality of condition previous to the (Revolutionary) war was, with few exceptions, in the same grade with themselves." She added that the airs assumed by men who had only recently held scythes or pounded anvils were obnoxious. Ordinary Americans, she recorded, held suspect those who might erect a government too splendid for the tastes and professions of the general population. And she left no doubt that those who had served as officers under George Washington were the men she meant.

In Washington's Continental Army, a first lieutenant was court-martialed and jailed because he demeaned himself by doing manual labor with a working detail of his men. Almost two centuries later, while stationed with the 1st Air Cavalry in the highlands of Vietnam, Air Force Maj. James I. Baginski, needed some housing for his small detachment of Air Force officers and enlisted people. The 1st Cavalry was busy and could not help much. The "Bagger" gave everyone some tools, "found" some lumber and, leading the work team himself, had the troops' quarters up and habitable in two days. Maj. Baginski later became Maj. Gen. Baginski and never lost the idea of "doing because it has to be done." Both actions were correct for the times and places.

Duty is the greatest regulator of the proper exercise of one's rights. Here we speak of duty as it was meant by Giuseppe Mazzini, Italy's great patriot of the early 19th century, when he said: "Every mission constitutes a pledge of duty. Every man is bound to consecrate his effort to its fulfillment. He will derive his rule of action from the profound conviction of that duty." The key to the high regard for duty flows naturally in that sense of proportion that we call common sense.

In times past, common sense often was at odds with the idea of dignity in officers. On balance, special privileges are relatively few and the responsibility great. Because this entire book's thrust is the fundamental responsibilities of officership, the following statement is worth repeating again and again: It is a paramount and overriding responsibility of every officer to take care of the people of the command (of whatever size) before caring for himself or herself. It is a cardinal principle. Yet some junior officers fail to understand that it requires a steadfast fidelity-not lip service-since the troops' loyalty cannot be commanded when they become embittered by selfish action.

Row deeply does the rule cut? In the line of duty, it cuts to the very bone. It is the officer's job to make sure that his or her people come first. Getting the short stick a time or two, if it happens, is part of the job.

Why take care of your people first and all of the time? The answer is elementary. It all comes back to the officer who cannot get by unless he is taken care of by his people, especially in combat. The close association and mutual support strengthens courage and self-confidence. Few, if any, are born with these qualities in full blossom. They are gifts from our ties with each other.

Last is the notion of accountability. Officers are accountable for what happens to the Armed Forces, their service and the people. If someone is sullying the uniform or obviously in need of some help, only the blindest and most insensitive officer will not take the tactful action necessary to correct the situation. This idea of accountability can be extended into the officer's wallet. Just as someone is responsible for every order given, someone is responsible if something breaks. If the order was a disaster or the thing broke because of some failing or stupidity on the part of the officer who gave the order or "broke it"-he or she may get to pay, in dollars and time.

4

Planning Your Career

No officer should be promoted who has not demonstrated the mental and physical stamina and the moral and physical courage required for greater responsibility.

-Gen. Dwight D. Eisenhower (during the North African campaign in 1943)

A main purpose of this book is to stimulate thought that will encourage officers to seek the truth about themselves. It is never a good idea to try to give precise formulas about things that, by nature, are indefinite and subject to many variable factors. Career planning is one such thing.

Career planning has only one basic rule. The individual officer is responsible for what happens to him or her. Essentially, it is much like the aphorism provided by Vice Adm. Ramsey about job progression, "It is not the job you have; it is the job you do that counts."

The military services provide exceptional education and training opportunities. Management systems clearly define job progression, responsibilities and a broad range of challenging specialties. The services also have experts to manage the careers of both officers and enlisted personnel. The focus of all this system of identification, career management and promotion is the individual. It will always be "what you do with the job you have" that will count.

People enter the military services for almost as many reasons as there are people. Some join because it is the only profession open at the time. Some are seeking educational opportunities. Many sign up for the "lure of the sea" or the opportunity to fly or the challenge of leading troops. Some come because they were unable to find a better job in the civilian world. Whatever the reason for entering, few come to military service with a firm determination and clear decision to serve a complete career.

Getting ahead is a matter of getting noticed. Getting noticed is an art. It has been called many things. "Positioning" is the latest term used to describe an officer who gets noticed by the powers that be. The easiest way to get noticed is to be beautiful if female or to stand 7 feet tall if male. Most of us fit neither of those categories; we must make it through life with the physique, physiognomy and failings with which we were born.

The absolute best way for an officer to become noticed is by simply doing the best job that he or she can. That doesn't involve the use of magic, and that doesn't mean getting a reputation for always being able to accomplish any job, even without the tools. (That reputation usually means that the officer is permitting some other people to get away with not doing their jobs.)

Generally, the first tour of service will solidify the decision to Attempt to serve a full career. If the newly commissioned officer is well-led, well-advised and given the opportunity to excel, the profession probably can gain another productive member. If, however, the newly commissioned officer is poorly led, given no opportunity to develop the fundamental skills and ethics necessary to the profession, and denied a chance to excel, the officer probably will leave the service with a bitter taste and unpleasant memories.

Forgotten all too often is that military officers eventually return to The civilian sector. When they do, and become everything from plumbers to politicians, they will always have an opportunity to affect the military services. Other than mandatory retirement, reasons for leaving the service are as diverse as reasons for joining. Often the primary reason is a perceived greater opportunity for the individual. Former officers' impact after they leave the service depends largely on the perception they had of their roles in the service.

Career progression differs among the services. Each has nuances that will enhance the possibility of progression. Most of these are well-covered in service-specific lore and publications.

There are no differences, however, among the services in the fundamental concepts of how to best enhance a career. The following rules apply to all:

* Do an exceptional job in whatever job you are given.
* Find out what you really enjoy doing; then find a way to do it.
* Become expert in your specific job; then take every opportunity to broaden yourself to qualify for a better job.
* Joint duty is mandatory and will extend your impact to the national level. An act of Congress now regulates "purple suit" staff assignments at the Department of Defense and its agencies. It is a mistake to attempt to avoid such assignments.
* Learn the system. If you wait for someone to do it to you, someone will! It is your profession, and the rules for that profession are very clearly spelled out by the individual services. If you don't know the rules, you can't play the game.

* Master the written and spoken word.

* The tools of destruction are important, but people make the system work. Know your people well. It is they who will make you.

* Ask for the job you want. Never ask to go from a job. Ask only to go to a better one.

* Your word is your bond; never thoughtlessly promise a favor.

* Do not attempt to be all things to all people. Be the best at what you are and what you are supposed to be.

* Volunteer frequently, but always thoughtfully.

* People like to have cheerful people around them. Be one of the cheerful.

* Lastly, always try to be a little bit better than you think you are. Don't be surprised when you are.

Many duties of an Armed Forces officer will require selfless dedication to difficult and unpleasant tasks. Do them well, but keep them in perspective. One great joy of the Armed Forces is that you will change jobs. Nothing-not even the good jobs-lasts forever.

When accomplishing the difficult, do it wisely. The profession is open about opportunity. Few, if any, service schools are designed to have students fail. Most are structured so that success is possible to anyone who will give his or her best. Row well an officer does in the school environment will bear strongly on performance in the duty environment.

Schools don't just happen. They reflect the perceived needs of each service. Every service has a listing of schools for itself and other services. This listing also tells how people get selected to attend. Find the listing and read it! Remember that while all schools teach things, they also afford an opportunity to increase the number of friends and acquaintances. That is probably the single biggest reason to try to get sent to any joint or allied school. If an officer is going to work in the joint and allied arenas, it is very useful to know and be known by the people.

The Irish have a saying, "If you don't ask, you can't get."

Joint and Allied Duty

The military officer is sworn to support and defend the Constitution and should take pride in the traditions and the uniform of his or her particular service. But it is the nation that commands first allegiance and defines duty. Because of this, part of an officer's duty will be served in national assignments with other services (joint duty) and with other nations (allied duty). Two benefits come from these kinds of assignments: They are becoming mandatory for promotion to senior rank, and they contribute immeasurably to personal growth and understanding of our world.

The photograph showing the Earth rising over the moon's horizon has been called the most important ever taken. It demonstrates that we all live on one small, but beautiful, planet. If, for now, we have only this single world, we must learn as much as possible about the people with whom we share the Earth. It is not vital that we always agree with them.

It would be nice if we could sit down with, and reason with, any people with whom we disagree on important matters. When faced with opponents or a society totally committed to your destruction, reason is not the first step in the process.

Learning about the people and systems on this planet is not a simple process, limited to occasional school courses. Rather, it is a life-long process. Winston Churchill is quoted as saying that the United States of America and Great Britain are two nations united by a common heritage and divided by a common language. Most of our allies do not even share the common language. How difficult will it be to understand people whose language does not include a concept for time or who are willing to wait generations to accomplish specific goals or ends? How can Americans function in an environment where the simple "come here" wave of a hand means exactly the opposite?

We tend to mark historical change in terms of four- or eight-year administrations. We can cope with people who are willing to wait genera-

tions only if we understand the historical background of such patience
and perseverance. That understanding requires both study and language
abilities. One must learn how to think in other frames of reference.

In bilingual dictionaries, the Russian word mir is always translated as
"peace." However, the concept behind the word means totally different
things in English and Russian. In Russian, it means a peace in which all
opposition to the central authority has been abandoned. It means an
agreement to submit to Soviet dominance in the mind of anyone educated
under the communist system. To the Western mind, "peace" is a condition in which both sides let each other alone to run their own lives. Not
quite the same thing!

American negotiators often have found that to their Russian counter-
parts, they were seen as devious indeed, since they asked for mir but
would not concede the need for acceptance of Soviet rules. Both Ambas-
sadors Paul Nitze and Edward Rowny have used the same phrase to explain this problem: "They don't always mean what they say." In the
Russian view, they mean exactly what they say.

The Armed Forces officer should attain fluency in at least one
language other than English and have some familiarity with several others
in order to extend greetings or warnings, for example. What languages
and what levels of proficiency are matters of choice and job. But to be
able to communicate only in English, because English is a standard for
aviation and some international corporate languages, is to be ineffective
in much of the world.

Sometimes, as in joint duty, even a command of American English will
be inadequate to understand the jargon of the other services.

Opportunities for joint duty are ample. The U.S. Space Command is
an example of one of the newer joint-assignment possibilities. Other
joint assignments range from the Joint Chiefs of Staff to small, single-
task units. Each directs and controls certain activities and programs of
our defense establishment. Personnel wear uniforms of their own services
and contribute to the common task according to the special skills they
bring from their parent service. The importance of joint duty is that it
is for national goals, not service-parochial goals. Joint duty is not a
challenge to make the specific service shine or to compete for service
domination.

Allied duty presents similar challenges, but differs in many ways. Other
nations' officers serving in allied assignments are more than mere symbols of their countries' cooperation. They expect to contribute as much
as any member of the staff and are usually there because of some special
skill or talent. In most cases, officers from the participating nations
are serving together as part of a single staff, with the same defense
goals. It takes only a short time for the open-minded newcomer to become a
func-

tioning part of the organization. The officer who cannot function as part of the team, however, will be quickly identified and sent packing to a less demanding assignment.

Overseas duty is as much a part of the profession as saluting and schooling. Every overseas job is important, or the nation would not have assigned an officer to the position. While there, the officer represents both the service and his or her country. Every action will be watched by the local population and the uniformed services of the host country. Local people may have preconceived and unflattering notions of America and Americans. Most of what the host-country citizens think they know about our society comes from the export of television and movies. What these media show is not always the way most Americans work, love and live. As a result, a service officer will be directly affecting the attitudes of many in the host country. You are, as the truism goes, an ambassador of the United States.

Seeing your paycheck's value fluctuate daily is a very powerful lesson in practical economics. Currency rates, trade balances and the impact of actions by other nations on service members and their capability to accomplish the mission tend to be academic concepts until one has lived them. We no longer live in "splendid isolation," and it is important to understand that few actions taken by any nation will occur in a vacuum. The price of tea in China will affect Bloomington, Ind., and the dollar's value fluctuations can constrain lifestyles of persons serving abroad.

Officers and others may have the opportunities to be accompanied by dependents. For many spouses and dependents, it may be the first opportunity to live in a different culture. That, in itself, presents both challenge and reward, and all officers must be sensitive to the problems posed by the transition from our culture to another. The Armed Forces have provided an extensive support system for service members and dependents. Schools, churches, Little League and libraries are but a few of these "touches of home." It is a different nation, however, and some younger spouses and dependents may have difficulty adjusting. Part of the overseas assignment will be to help people adapt. Above all, do the homework necessary to make sure that proposed actions are going to work in the host country.

Do not emulate the action officer some years ago in Europe who was given the task of finding a new base for B-52 bombers. He researched the problem carefully and came up with two options. Both were well-examined; either would work. He had accounted for all contingencies: people, housing, equipment, fuel, schools, churches and local reaction.

He presented his findings to the senior staff and made a recommendation to use Base A. The staff agreed and made a formal recommendation to the commander, who passed it on to U.S. headquarters where it was approved for presentation to the host-country government. Presentations to various levels of the host-country government went very well until he was asked: "Major, what is that little black square just off the end of the runway?" The questioner was the deputy minister for internal affairs in the host country.

The major looked closely at the map and told the minister that it was a house.

"Whose house is it, major?" the minister asked quietly. The major fumbled a bit and finally admitted that he did not know.

"It is my house, major, and it will be a cold day in the nether regions when you fly B-52s over my house at 50 feet in the air.

"Request for the use of the base is denied!"

Keeping Your House in Order

An officer lives in the real world and can expect real-world problems.
Computer operators will err, checks will bounce, paperwork will get lost,
and everything that happens to a civilian will happen to the officer.
Vulnerable to the worst of both worlds, the Armed Forces officer straddles
a stream with slippery banks. Moving around the world on a frequent basis
means re-establishing banking relationships and being the new guy on the
block with the low-numbered checks.

Computer credit checks are making it much simpler to establish credit
in a new location. It is the officer's responsibility to ensure that the
report is accurate and up-to-date. The only other person who will really
care if the report is accurate tends to be a supervisor or commander who
gets a call or letter. The Armed Forces understand that bad things can
happen to good people and have a certain tolerance for the possibility of
human error. The other side of that particular coin is that being commissioned an officer reduces this tolerance to almost zero. Aesop's story
about the squirrel who spent most of the summer scurrying to store up
nuts for the winter is especially appropriate for Armed Forces officers.
Just as one cannot talk sense to a person who has been bitten by the new-
car bug, it is difficult to convince many people of the need for saving on
a regular basis.

A cash reserve is important. So is the discipline of understanding that
emergencies will happen. It is natural and normal to want the amenities
of life. According to many TV shows and popular magazines, it is abnormal not to have the good things now.

Large bureaucratic institutions such as banks and the Armed Forces do
not run on word-of-mouth. They run on documentation. The documentation can be stored electronically or on paper, but the nature of the beast
is that it is up to the individual to make sure the documentation is
correct and there. Rarely will anyone be given only one copy of any order
or supporting document.

File the documents. All record-keeping Systems are fallible, and it is not unheard of for records to become lost. The burden of proof is always on the officer. Having a copy can prove it happened.

Making a will is basic good business. It is a fundamental step which once taken, allows time for more important considerations. Everyone is going to die at some time. In the event of a sudden death, a formal will makes the management of the estate much easier for both family and the estate officer. Death has been described as the "maker of instant trash" that family and friends will have to wade through to find the important things. If for some private reason it is determined to exclude the next of kin from this listing, it could be kept in the office, deposited with a lawyer or an insurance agent so that it will surface after the officer's death. Every officer also should have a full and complete inventory of his or her holdings, interests, obligations, insurance and receivables.

By the profession's nature, an officer may spend a great deal of time away from home and hearth. It may be useful to execute powers of attorney so that normal and abnormal situations can be handled during that absence. These can be drawn up by the legal office, and, most importantly, the personnel of that office will explain what can happen when the power of attorney is granted to the wrong person.

Developing an inventory of household goods is time-consuming and tedious. It is also a life-saver when the packers lose a box or drop Aunt Mabel's antique dining-room table. Without this inventory, claims for damage or loss just will not fly. For items of special value, it is a good idea to have their photographs on file.

Insurance is a necessity for any officer. The type, kind and amount are matters of personal judgment that depend on circumstance. Services do not try to tell anyone how much insurance should be provided. Insurance needs can best be met by professionals. The variety of modern insurance programs and the Tax Reform Act of 1986 have created an opportunity to develop an insurance-based program of substantive and real value.

Allotments are a blessing, providing a simple, painless way to make sure that recurring expenses never fall through the crack. Each service has special rules and procedures for making out an allotment. All are simple and remove one more irritant from the day-to-day business of life. An allotment reserves a specific amount to be sent to a savings account or a named recipient.

Spouses are an important part of the total fabric of the Armed Forces. They can enhance lives and careers. Much of the Armed Forces structure is dedicated to meeting family members' needs for growth, personal satisfaction and development. But they are not in the service. Decisions about subordinates, lifestyles and careers could include inputs from spouses, but in the final analysis, the officer must make the decisions.

7

Where Is the Real Service?

"What we have is a school situation. Things will be different in the real service." Or, "This is not the real force. Just wait until you get there."

Just where is the real service? Just where is it that the mission takes priority and paperwork takes a back seat to getting the job done? It's right here, right now.

The Armed Forces' real mission takes place wherever a service member is assigned. There are no back seats, no non-essential functions, no slide by jobs and no room in the Armed Forces for anyone who thinks there are. Every job is important and worth one's time and best effort.

It may not seem like it at the time. The job may be boring and not demand full skills and talents. It may even seem like a waste of time. It isn't. The Armed Forces function because every job, apparently meaningful or not, gets done to the best of the performer's ability.

Air Force Gen. William W. (Spike) Momyer made few friends with maintenance people in Vietnam. He would fire aircraft crew chiefs right and left for having time-honored "private" stocks of critical parts. Few understood, at the time, that his goal was not to punish people for taking the extra step to meet the mission demands. He understood that the system had to function with every little piece working to its fullest. He believed that every crew chief with a "private" stock of scrounged parts detracted from the capability of the entire logistics system to meet the needs of the combat forces.

The Navy's goal of putting ordnance on target has the same basic problem as did Gen. Momyer. If everyone does the job properly, the system will function and it will be possible to get the ordnance on target. If, for the want of a nail, a battle will be lost, then the system needs changing. The Armed Forces have demonstrated an ability to respond quickly to the mission's changing demands. However, as a system, they must understand when some part of the system is not working properly.

It took a presidential directive to force the Ordnance Department to accept repeating rifles. The rifles were clearly superior and a significant technological advance for the time. The issue was ammunition consumption. The Ordnance Department complained, "If we give them plenty of bullets, they will just shoot them up."

While the logic or illogic of the major problems is seemingly apparent at all levels of command, what relationship does this have to the newly commissioned officer buried in a corner desk at post headquarters or China Lake or up on the DEW Line or reviewing requisitions at some Coast Guard station? How can that officer have an impact on "the real service?" By setting the standards for duty performance, integrity, honor and example for that desk, section, location or group of people. No matter how much it may seem like it, there are very few Camp Swampys in the Armed Forces. An officer may be surrounded by people who have been allowed to become apathetic or unconcerned about their skill levels or their readiness. The challenge is to change things. Set the standard.

It is never easy to be willing to stand out and maintain the standards. But, who else will? The other guy is just that, the other guy.

8

Getting Along With People

*No one likes a perverse, obstinate person: everyone speaks scornfully of
him and avoids him.*

-The Yamana Code of Behavior

Neither peace nor wars are won through ideology. Both are won or
lost by human beings. The human is a strange beast. It will live or die
based on what it thinks of itself. What people think of themselves is
dependent upon what others think of them! Paradoxical? Not really.
People will respond pretty much the same way they are treated.

One clear proposition about getting along with people is this: "If you
like people, if you seek contact with them rather than hiding in a corner,
if you study your fellow man sympathetically, if you try consistently to
contribute something to their success and happiness, if you are reasonably generous with your thoughts and your time, if you have a partial
reserve with everyone but a seeming reserve with no one, if you work to
be interesting rather than spend to be a good fellow, you will get along
with your superiors, your subordinates, your roommate and the human
race."

It is easy to chart a course for the individual who is wise enough to
make human relations a prime concern. Getting the knack of it is a different story. More has been written about human relations than on any
other subject. Since Confucius' time, great and lesser minds have
addressed the guidance of personal conduct. The odd part of all of this
effort is that the major causes for friction in modern society still come
from individual feelings of inferiority, false pride, vanity,
unwillingness to yield space to another and the consequent urge to throw
one's weight around.

A cynic once said, "Never appeal to a man's higher nature. He may
not have one! Always appeal to his self-interest; there you may have a
chance!"

While that may seem too pragmatic and too basic, it isn't!

People are motivated by many things. The first and strongest motivation is self-interest. Try to tell a pregnant woman, deep in the throes of childbirth, that her baby could become president of the United States, and she will clearly define your immediate genealogy. However, give her a few days to recover and imprint with her child and she will give a different answer. Similarly, a major role of the Armed Forces is to get beyond the immediate pain of basic training and to teach the subordination of self for the greater good of the nation.

One view of the way to get along with people is the quote published in the United States Coast Guard magazine under the title Thirteen Mistakes. The article said it is a mistake:

1. To attempt to set up your own standard of right and wrong.

2. To try to measure the enjoyment of others by your own.

3. To expect uniformity of opinions in the world.

4. To fail to make allowance for inexperience.

5. To endeavor to mold all dispositions alike.

6. Not to yield on unimportant trifles.

7. To look for perfection in our own actions.

8. To worry ourselves and others about what cannot be remedied.

9. Not to help everybody wherever, however and whenever we can.

10. To consider impossible what we cannot ourselves perform.

11. To believe only what our finite minds can grasp.

12. Not to make allowances for the weakness of others.

13. To estimate by some outside quality, when it is that within which makes the person.

The unobserving officer perhaps will dismiss the list as just so many cliches. The reflective one will accept it as a negative guide to positive conduct; it engages practically every principle vital to the growth of a strong spiritual life when relating to people.

All too frequently, people make permanent conclusions about other people based on snap judgments and either write them off or limit the ability to help them. In a complex, crowded world, the lack of time to assess fully the potential of others requires some kind of discriminator. The Armed Forces have such a discriminator. It is a fast, effective tool that does not rely on sex, race or religion. It exists on the sleeve, shoulder or collar of every member of the Armed Forces. It is a clear statement of capability and the right to be there as an equally valuable member of the Armed Forces.

When a person brings to a new unit a bad efficiency report, that fact should be noted with mild interest and no prejudice. A new assignment means a clean slate, with no overhang from what has happened, including possibly mistaken judgment of others. To be perpetually doubted is an impossible situation that destroys confidence and creates personal fear and discontent. A person is entitled to a fresh hold on security with a new superior. Any wise and experienced senior commander can cite numerous examples of people who were sent to him with spotty records and an understandable nervousness about the future. As soon as they realized that they were not going to get another kick, they improved and went on to become superior performers. For any right-minded officer, it should be far more gratifying to salvage and restore human material than to take over an organization that is sound from top to bottom.

The studied effort to be helpful in all relations with people and to give help not grudgingly, but cheerfully, courteously and in greater measure than is expected is the fast lane to wide influence and personal strength of character. More than all else, the little kindnesses in life bind people together.

Other than these comments, it is unnecessary to discuss at great length the inner qualities that give an officer the easy adjustment to other people in all walks of life. It is well to remember the importance of enthusiasm, cheerfulness, kindness, courtesy and justice, which are the safeguards of honor and the tokens of mutual respect between people. All are important as people go forward together, prosper in each other's company and find strength in the bonds of mutual service.

Anyone's reputation is formed largely by what others see on the outside. In the military service, manners play a major role for several reasons. First, the uniform invariably makes the wearer conspicuous. Second, the public expects the officer to look the part of an officer. Officers are expected to embody character, be given to clear and friendly speech, be capable of expressing ideas with respectful assurance and enthusiasm and be careful of customs and good usage while carrying themselves with poise and humor. Unless they present an aura of vitality, confidence and reflection that is assumed of a leader, they will be suspected of not being leaders. However unfair that judgment might seem in relation to other professions, it has a logical basis. People will excuse wide variations of dress and behavior in many professions without becoming concerned about national defense. When the same people see any member of the Armed Forces acting in an uncivil manner or unkempt in any way, they assume the Armed Forces are going to the dogs. One reason for the Marine Corps' prestige is that the public rarely, if ever, sees a sloppy Marine. What they do see is the reflection of morale and esprit that is common to all members of the Armed Forces, but perhaps most visible in Marines.

9

Leadership

If you lead the people through virtue and regulate them by the laws of propriety, then they will have a sense of honor and shame and will attain goodness.

-Confucius

Any leadership book must come to grips with the fundamentals. What is leadership? Can it be learned or taught? At what point is one supposed to be a leader? These are but a few of the basic questions that should occur to any young officer. There are many, many more questions and just as many books, pamphlets and courses that will examine the details of leadership. All are readily available, and some of the best are incorporated into the various service professional schools.

We cannot all be a Grant, turning the tide of the war by simply pointing the troops back to the battle with a wave of a hand from atop his horse. Nor can we be a Washington the indomitable, a Patton the philosopher, a Mahan the visionary or a MacArthur the fearless. No, we must be ourselves.

Leadership has two elements: a leader and a follower. What makes leaders and followers is the magic that makes any armed force work.

Why would people follow a 13-year-old boy or, for that matter, a 14-year-old girl and think they could make history?

The boy was Genghis Khan and the girl, Joan of Arc. They changed the map of the world. They had something that made people follow and become willing to die for their beliefs.

We have had leaders from all molds. Some have been controlled by fear, some made things happen by love and devotion, and some made things happen because of the respect they held for their people. One of the better modern generals has a reputation for making nothing happen, at least on the surface!

"When you have a problem-send Warren! It never seems like he does all that much, but wherever he goes, things work right!"

Work right it usually did. At one point during the national turmoil over involvement in Vietnam, a very vocal woman's group telephoned the base that Air Force Col. Warren Moore (later major general) commanded and announced its intention to totally disrupt flight operations as a protest. No one really knows what the women expected. We can tell you what they got! Col. Moore invited the women to come and protest, and he promised that he would personally walk with them so that they could "reason together" without interference. His staff members were deeply concerned about image and reaction if his actions were misunderstood by the press and the base.

They were unaware that Col. Moore had served under a commanding general who had set an example of true leadership. That general, when faced with overt racism at a supporting base, had called in the press to watch as he fired the base commander for permitting racism to flourish.

August in Arizona is hot. Tarmac soaks up the heat in a hurry. Col. Moore met the protest group at the front gate and escorted them directly to the flight line. He walked with them out onto the tarmac and to one of the main taxiways. He stopped and sat down on the taxiway motioning all of the ladies to join him and block the taxiway.

August, hot tarmac and thin summer dresses do not mix well. The entire group left for the front gate, some burn ointment and a better time to protest. Col. Moore went back to his office, took the copy of Life out of his pants and called the major commander to report, "no problem, no protest, no publicity."

Often the first question asked is if there is any difference between management skills and leadership. Debate has raged for a long time. Direct combat commanders most often respond with a firm "no," and support people tend to say "yes."

Both are correct. The most succinct perspective was provided by retired Army Lt. Gen. John E Forrest, who has been both a combat commander and a senior staff manager. "You manage bullets, and you lead people. Both skills are required of an officer, and the very best officers know when to use each skill."

The Armed Forces believe that both management and leadership skills can be learned and will provide ample opportunity for both academic and hands-on development. Being a junior officer involves primarily learning, developing skills and being afforded the opportunity to demonstrate enough proficiency and knowledge to be given greater responsibility. In no other profession will the opportunity for large responsibility be offered as quickly. In no other profession will a leader be as trusted. This is true for both commissioned officers and non-commissioned officers. It is the essence and the beauty of American Armed Forces.

Most other nations and societies are not so blessed. They expend considerable effort just making sure the limited trust given to the services is continually watched and monitored. In our Armed Forces, we assume and expect trust, responsibility and accountability from all service members.

What are the common denominators of leadership? Many of our past great leaders have shared them. First is the ability to inspire trust and confidence. This does not result from a single act, braid on your sleeve or time in service. It starts with the demonstration of a command of the craft. It matters not whether the craft is artillery, boat handling, flying or whatever. The officer's ability to demonstrate proficiency and knowledge will start to inspire people. They will willingly follow orders if they believe that the officer is going to be right.

A second key and common ingredient of leadership is integrity. When an officer demonstrates that every action is based on duty and the right thing to do and that no personal gain is the reason for the action, people will follow willingly. The concept of integrity includes personal courage. Courage can be defined in a number of ways peculiar to the situation. It can be argued that courage under combat conditions cannot be known until combat. That may well be true, but much of the time in the profession will not be spent in direct combat. What kind of courage is meaningful during these non-combat times? Courage of conviction, courage to stand up for the rights of people, courage of decision and the courage to be wrong and admit it are a few that can be demonstrated daily. The coin's opposite side is a foolhardy brashness that charges windmills. An officer who establishes a reputation for hard-headed and simplistic bull-in-a-china-shop approaches to leadership will soon cause followers to stay way, way in the rear.

Just as some armies would demonstrate courage by having officers walk nonchalantly up and down the battle lines, troops will judge an officer in battle not only by personal courage but also by his knowledge of the science of ballistics. There is a time to take the hill and a time to keep heads down!

Leadership is communication. Demonstration of knowledge, integrity, duty and courage is a part of this process. So is the ability to listen and to direct action. Listen first! Nature provided two eyes, two ears and one mouth. Use them in that ratio. By demonstrating the basics of leadership, an officer learns that the people working with him or her have information that will help to make the right decision. All information is based on perspective. It may be accurate and correct as far as it goes. Part of the leader's job is to collect all of the information and act.

Leadership means accepting the fact that one may make some enemies along the way. When it is necessary, remember well the advice of the sage who warned us to choose our enemies more carefully than our friends.

Leadership is warranted ego. Leaders actively seek responsibility and power because they believe they can do the job well. Sometimes, ego is all the political candidate has to offer. Yet, once elected, the individual often grows to fill the job. Ego, balanced by humility, causes a George Washington-on the eve of his inauguration-to say, "I am probably the least well-equipped man in the room to take this job."

Leadership is the vision to keep the forest in sight when everyone else is seeing trees. The talent to gain and keep perspective is an essential ingredient of leadership. That perspective led an ex-artillery captain to the conclusion that the dismissal of General of the Army Douglas A. MacArthur could not be couched in cosmetics, when he said it was a decision of such importance that it could only be made by the president of the United States.

Leadership is innovation. It is a sense of timing and the willingness to put a new idea to work. Innovation based on knowledge makes innovation the middle name of successful leaders. General of the Army Dwight D. Eisenhower put it in these words: "The commander's success will be measured more by his ability to lead than his adherence to fixed notions."

Leadership is encouraging people to believe in themselves and how good they really can be.

It is the magic that the Marines call command presence. It is an indefinable combination of ingredients. It is not size nor demeanor nor sex nor physique that has people identifying leadership in others. The closest description we can offer is the almost Victorian concept of competence and integrity so strong that they show on the outside. This cannot be learned, only lived.

A few governing principles help to address the problem of generating greater powers of leadership among officers. It is easy to say, "Do this" or "Do that" or "Be this" or "Be that." For most people the question is not so much "what" but "how?"

One school of thought holds that the Armed Forces have so much in common with industry that both systems can be successfully "managed" with the same skills and techniques. The same school of thought believes all things to be quantifiable, measurable and rational. To gain perspective, we have only to read any Armed Forces' citation for heroism.

People are led, and things are managed. Very few board meetings, production lines, advertising or sales meetings require that people be willing to die. Few combat situations can be plotted on a program evaluation and technique chart. Management, like politics, is the art of consensus and accommodation to the possible. Leadership is the art of creating a willing followership for a common cause that may appear impossible. An Armed Forces officer will find need of both skills. Only a few will become "great captains," but all can be leaders.

The Mission

The word "mission" is especially appropriate to the Armed Forces and implies something beyond the call of duty. Achievement of United States' aims involves much more than simply giving and carrying out correct orders with promptness and intelligence.

The Armed Forces system reflects inherent frailties and limitations of humans who make up the system. No single officer of any rank or experience can understand all nuances of a given problem, make correct judgments on every aspect of possible weakness and then write a perfect analysis and solution. The officer can come close, but will always need help from the rest of the system. It is only when everyone in the system takes personal responsibility for the general well-being of the system that the system will meet the demand of the "mission."

In a literal sense, one is not "in" the Armed Forces, one "is" the Armed Forces. The chairman of the Joint Chiefs of Staff and the 0-1 buried in the frozen wasteland of the Arctic Circle are the service and have an obligation to make that service as good as it can be. The old adage "If it ain't broke, don't fix it" has a corollary that should be stamped on the ID card of every officer. It goes like this: "If it is broken, fix it or find the person who can."

Rank has nothing to do with "fixing broken stuff." In every war; we have had examples of very junior officers developing ideas, concepts and even tactics that made significant differences.

The most successful single-day MiG sweep in the entire Vietnam War was the result of a young F-4 back-seater being able to apply the classic story of the Trojan Horse to aerial operations. The radio call signs of bombers and fighter escorts had become so predictable that the North Vietnamese could tell, just by listening to the radio, which types of attack aircraft were en route. Bombers were slower; more heavily laden and easier targets for what had become a very sophisticated air defense system. Fighter escorts carried bombs that could be jettisoned as soon as it was apparent that the MiGs were becoming a threat to the bombers. When they did jettison, they turned the forest into toothpicks, but did little damage to actual enemy targets. Either way, the MiGs had accomplished the main goal of keeping bombs off target.

On one specific day, the entire force used only bomber call signs, and there wasn't a bomb on a single plane! All were loaded with air-to-air weapons. The MiGs came up to play and promptly screamed foul as seven of them were shot down.

Many more examples help to make the point that every member of the Armed Forces has some responsibility for the state of the Armed Forces. It is every person, taking the time and making the effort to get the small things right and learning how to think and act in more serious circumstances, that will make the mission a success.

When an order is given, what does it mean to the person who receives it? The sequence given by Brig. Gen. S.L.A. Marshall is this:
1. To be certain that he understands what is required.
2. To examine and organize the required resources as promptly as possible.
3. To execute the order without waste of time or means.
4. To call for support if events prove that the means are inadequate.
5. To fill up the spaces in the orders if there are developments that had not been anticipated.
6. When the job is done, to prepare to go on to something else.

Dr. Larry Fogel, a logic consultant to the Department of Defense, put it a little differently. He suggested that the first question when dealing with problems in a bureaucracy is, "Is this my problem, or does it belong to someone else?" Once that question has been answered, one needs to determine the root of the problem. Why did it surface now, and what is the real question? Once those answers are in hand, one can begin to find and solve the problem and carry out the orders.

Few things will warm the heart of a superior as much as the subordinate who understands the first time, salutes smartly and gets the job done. This kind of person is a jewel beyond price and well worth marking for bigger things. On the other hand, most of us take more than one quick order to understand fully what is required. A fascinating and unique trait of American Armed Forces members is that they want to know why something is being done. Once they understand the why of a situation, they will give it their best shot.

Given time, it is just as important to explain the order as it is to give it. It makes no sense to be impatient or resentful that you had to explain the order. Orders are not always clear; and people do not always listen well. It is important for officers to think and to be able to present ideas or orders in a clear, understandable manner.

Timing is just as important as getting the mission done in a prompt and positive way. Just as there is a time to live, a time to love and a time to die, there is a time for action and a time to think. Pity the superior whose people rush madly into action!

The idea of disobeying orders is difficult to handle. When does an officer say no? It is, after all, a grave crime to disobey a lawful order within the military. It makes no difference that the order may seem to be dumb or stupid or even incomprehensible. If it is legal, it must be obeyed! Only when the order is unlawful and obviously a crime must it be disobeyed.

What happens when the subordinates tell a superior that the order is not illegal, but is wrong? Does that mean that the superior must change the order? Far from it! It means only that the superior should re-evaluate the order and come to a decision about its validity. If it is wrong, the superior must change it! If, however, it is right, the pressure from below must not influence the decision. Given time, only the most arrogant, selfcentered superiors will not provide an opportunity for the views and opinions of subordinates to be heard, evaluated and acted upon. However, it is each officer who has been given "special trust and confidence." A staff is useful, but the officer gets paid to take the heat and make the decision.

The first secretary of defense, James Forrestal, gave small, printed wall plaques to officers serving in some joint intelligence offices in the Pentagon. The message: "A person's judgment is only as good as the information on which it is based." When he visited those officers, he looked for that message on the wall.

Decision makers, civilian or military, can act only on the information they have been given. The information may be unpleasant or unwelcome. We could all do well to remember the answer given by the commander of a fighter training squadron when a national emergency arose and he was asked to give the status of his forces. "I have six shooters and five rammers." That was not the expected response, and the duty officer in the command post asked what it meant. The commander replied, "I have six aircraft with guns and five more who will use their aircraft as weapons if needed."

The attitude differs sharply from that of the general who was asked the secret of his success. He responded that he had gotten to the top rank of his service by never taking on a fight he did not know he could win.

The courage to start and the courage to take a risk make the difference that defines a few great captains. That does not eliminate the need for collecting data, evaluating the situation and estimating the probable out-comes. In every situation, there is the moment for action. The action may involve risk and the potential for failure, but whatever action is taken should be based on the best available information and begun with the simple, courageous act of beginning.

11

Knowing Your Job

War is too serious a matter to be taught by the inexperienced.
                                                    -Robert Heinlein

C lose enough for government work" gets people killed! One of those killed might well be you. There is no excuse for any officer not to have mastered the assigned job. Perfection is not the immediate goal for the junior officer, but mastery of the job is.

The Armed Forces fully understand that all new officers are novices and need to learn. Rarely will the new officer find the crusty curmudgeon who delights in showing how little both he and the new officer know. Most officers understand the need to teach and help the novice become a professional and do so willingly. The comment that "second lieutenant is the best rank in the military. They are the only officers who ain't sup- posed to know nothing. They are supposed to make mistakes" does little for the ego of the second lieutenant, but it can be a fair-if flippant- statement.

The condition is not terminal. An officer will be expected to learn and grow in ability at a rate that continues to astonish and amaze the most jaded educators. Even though a novice, he or she still is an officer and will be given exceptional responsibility and accountability as worthiness is established. The Armed Forces will provide the framework and the sup- port necessary for the officer to learn as fast as possible.

Truth is that there is never any assignment, no matter how undemand- ing, that entitles an Armed Forces officer to waste any working hours of the day. The range of study required to master the profession is so great and so complex that every wasted minute puts the officer hours behind in knowledge and probably behind on the promotion list. Almost any senior officer will be quick to point out that the higher one goes, the more study is required just to keep abreast. The world is changing for them, too.

Not all wisdom is found in books. This is most true when just breaking into the Armed Forces. Novices in any field are expected to ask questions, questions and more questions. Wisdom begins at the point of
understanding that the only thing shameful about ignorance is staying
that way by choice! One major difference between the familiar soil of
civilian life and the terra incognita of military life is the lack of
familiarity, the sweeping environmental change. The new officer doesn't
understand the system that makes things work, who are the real powers and
why things happen as they do. Everyone in the Armed Forces can give the
new officer helpful information.

Study of human nature and the Armed Forces will consume considerable time in this profession. Everything becomes grist for the curiosity
mill. If Ardant du Picq is correct when he says "the heart of man does
not change," your interest must focus on human nature. Whatever can be
learned for certain about the nature of man as a fighting animal can be
filed for ready reference; the hour will come when it will be useful.

Ideally, an officer should be able to do the work of anyone serving
under that officer. We do not live in an ideal world. Our system has become so complex and technical that, except for the most simple situations, the ideal cannot be achieved with any hope of getting the job done.
It is critical, however, that the officer know the job and demonstrate an
understanding of the work problems that concern the subordinates, so
that effective command is possible.

What kind of knowledge is the officer expected to possess? A realistic
view is found in the distinction between the power to do a job well and to
be able to determine when it is well done.

Adjustment to, and mastery of, a military officer's job comes from per-
sistent pursuit of that principle. The main technique is study and constant re-examination of criteria. To correctly measure the standards of
performance as to the value of the work and the ability of the personnel,
one must become immersed in the nature and purpose of all operations.

There is no shortcut. Patient application to one thing at one time is
the first rule of success. All specialists like to talk about their work.
Interest in that work is flattering, and everyone grows in knowledge by
Simply picking people's brains. Paths to informed judgment are book
study, specialized courses, informed comments by superiors and
subordinates and human experience. It is, as is science, "organized
common sense."

All things being equal, the prospect for any officer's progress will be
determined by attitude. It is the receptive mind, rather than the oracle,
that inspires confidence. Gen. Eisenhower said at one point that after 40
years, he still thought of himself as a student and he consciously mis-
trusted any man who believed he had the full and final answer to problems that, by their nature, are ever-changing.

To rule by work rather than to work by rules must be the abiding principle in military operations. Peacetime accountability for the smallest

screw is part of the job and may even make sense. In time of war, the job is not to count screws but to accomplish the mission with the minimum loss of life. Making sure that the screws are in the right place at the right time is important, but there is no real economy in war other than that which keeps the blood in people's bodies, not on the ground.

Ruling by work will make accountants unhappy. It also will require that possibly unpopular decisions be made. Army Gen. William C. Westmoreland decided to use the ships bringing military supplies to Vietnam as floating warehouses, in spite of the exceptionally high demurrage charges, for one simple reason. It got the troops into battle without an extensive base-support infrastructure. It was not a popular decision, but one made with the mission in mind. And that is what the officer's job is all about.

Another aspect to knowing the job goes beyond the bounds of the Armed Forces. We are a part of the larger nation and, when called to war; use the full resources of the nation. We employ everything that can be used for a military purpose to increase training and fighting efficiency. Doing this requires a continuing meeting of the minds between military leadership and the leaders and experts of a wide range of skills and disciplines in the nation as a whole. Each side must understand the other's capabilities. Each must recognize the real and imagined limitations of education, economics, production, resources and-most importantly-will.

We once viewed as limitless the resources and capabilities of the nation. In a much smaller world of almost infinite complexity, reality has tempered this optimistic view. Just as children are taught that the family bud- get cannot include some items, we as a nation now understand that there are things that cannot be had. This does not mean inadequate defense, training or capability. It does mean that the Armed Forces and the individual officer must understand both the full richness and potential of the nation and the realistic limits to that potential and will.

A last thought on knowing the job: There is more to be discovered about training, management and combat command than has ever been learned.

Writing and Speaking

Mastery of self-expression is one difference between the competent and the exceptional. All things being equal, the officer who has expended the effort to master the skills of writing and speaking will rise more rapidly, be a more effective leader and contribute more to the military service and the nation.

History is full of examples of clear, concise statements that have been used with great effect. Any Latin student will recall the words used by Julius Caesar to describe his conquest of an entire nation. ("Veni, vidi, vici" -"I came, I saw, I conquered.")

World War II Army Brig. Gen. Anthony C. McAuliffe used only on word in response to the German request for surrender. Outgunned, 0' manned and surrounded at Bastogne, McAuliffe's response was a simple statement of American determination in the face of apparently impossible odds: "Nuts!"

In recorded military history, mastery of communication has been a mark of the successful military officer. Ability to impart information in a clear, concise manner is a blessing for both superiors and subordinates. Superiors already overburdened with a mass of sometimes conflicting information welcome the discovery of an officer who can present an oral or written case that is logical, brief and to the point. That officer will always be able to get a hearing.

For the subordinate who needs either directions or information, it is an equal blessing to find a superior who can provide clear information in an understandable manner. Most people neither need nor want long, detailed expositions of grand strategy. They simply want to know what they are supposed to do now.

Many years ago, President Calvin Coolidge reportedly listened to one of the day's great evangelists, who spoke more than two hours on a very hot summer morning about the sinful nature of man. He waxed poetic on the nature and consequences of sin and on each person's responsibility to avoid sinful situations.

When the president finally returned home, his wife-who had not attended the service-was curious.

"Calvin," she said, "what was the sermon about?"
"Sin," replied the president, as he continued to rock in his chair.
"Well," she said in exasperation, "what did he have to say about it?"
"He's agin' it," Coolidge replied.

We cannot be certain the story is true, but we do know that Disraeli was correct when he noted that "Men govern through words." Governments govern by words, and battles are won through the ability of people to express concrete ideas in clear, unmistakable language. In the Armed Forces, command is exercised through written and oral communication that must be articulate and understandable at all levels.

The proliferation of computer-managed command and control systems, automated reporting and accounting systems and other mechanical aids to the management and command of the military forces fails to diminish the need for excellence in written and oral communications skills.

Rather, it makes it all the more important. Once officers understand that clear, concise articulation of orders, information and directives is a basic requirement, the exceptional officer will accept the corollary: Superior qualification in use of the written and spoken words is as essential to military leadership as the knowledge of the whole technique of weapons handling and the use of complex systems.

It then becomes a matter of personal decision whether the officer will develop the communications skills necessary for exceptional leadership or will hide behind the excuse offered by too many, "I have no gift for writing or speaking."

How often have you heard this flimsy excuse? How often have you inferred that the speaker derives a perverse pride from what amounts to self-inflicted ignorance? It is similar to the flight instructor who is so busy teaching flying that there is no time for shining flight boots; he may be the best flight instructor since Orville and Wilbur Wright started the whole business of aviation. Unfortunately, such a slovenly instructor misses the point about the total array of skills and abilities that make up the professional military officer. He has a responsibility to teach more than flying. He also must teach the equally vital concept that officers, by the fact of being officers, must set all of the standards of conduct and behavior all day, every day. In the very same way, officers are expected to set the standard in communications skills.

The author of a command and staff school pamphlet on plain talk and readable writing used the acronym KISS as a memory tickler: "Keep It Simple, Stupid!"

Not all American military leaders have been experts at polishing a phrase or giving concise, succinct guidance or orders. But the majority who have excelled in leadership have also made a mark in the field of letters. A sampler of just some American military leaders who have also been exceptional communicators of ideas ranges from Washington to Grant to Eisenhower to Marshall to Eaker. In modern times, retired general officers have penned magazine articles and newspaper columns to bring understanding of defense issues to millions of non-military Americans.

To put this skill into some kind of perspective, look at any hate-mongering literature in this or any other country. From our point of view, the material is offensive to most thinking people, and it is stupid. Mere publication of the material, however, will convince some people that it is correct. All great religions, philosophies and governing systems depend on the written word to convince people that a particular point of view is necessary and right.

Writing

How does one become a good writer?

Anyone who has the brains to gain a commission has the brains to become a good writer. It requires work. It doesn't come easily or quickly. It demands time and effort to master the language. It demands practice, practice and more practice. Lastly, the writer must have something to say. The task is to deliver the message of substance in the clearest possible way. Almost always this means the shortest way.

A person who reads a lot soon finds that writing is almost as easy as reading. Most effective officers read a lot, and not just instruction manuals.

The only way to become a writer is to write. There are reasons why the services are so free with dictionaries and run so many courses on fundamental writing skills. There are reasons why the services have either published or adopted a manual style and format. The services want to provide opportunities for mastery of the language. Just as a condition of the profession demands that an officer master a particular weapon, learning the language of the profession is similarly essential. Poor spelling, poor grammar and lack of specific vocabulary are excuses, not the result of effort. Even great athletes, whose stock in trade is essentially muscular coordination, understand the need for practice.

In the same way, good writing comes from practice and practice and more practice. Only after the process of making words into sentences and sentences into paragraphs and paragraphs into chapters becomes a natural rhythmic process does the stamp of individuality and personality shine through the writing to the reader.

Extensive practice creates the ability to look at a problem, define its important parts and discover the possible solutions. Before one can write, one has to think. What an officer thinks will be reflected in the structure, the choice of words and the logic of the writing. This does not mean that the task will ever become easy. Good writing always will require more perspiration than inspiration.

While this may sound formidable, it is one key to professional progress and is worth the effort. One delight of the Armed Forces is the range of topics that are directly applicable to the service and mission.

Brig. Gen. S.L.A. Marshall said that the military establishment is a better school for writing than any other organization in our society. Unlike the literary critic who does nothing but express a personal perception of how well an author may or may not have done, military writing results in action. It needs no critic to determine if the results are good or bad.

Churchill had a "gift" of forceful expression as did MacArthur. In both cases, the "gift" was the direct result mastering the language and years of dedicated practicing and rewriting. Both of these masters of the written word had something to say. It was based on their study of great ideas and the presentation of these great ideas by other masters of the language. Both were familiar with the ideas that control the destiny of man and nations. They also incorporated into their writing the techniques that had been used effectively to present these ideas.

Substance is essential to military writing. In the world of the arts, it is frequently in vogue to praise style and ignore substance. This is unacceptable in writing for the Armed Forces. There is a wealth of literature about the world's armed forces, and some of the best is given at the end of this book. Because of the diversity of the services and the specific interests of the officer corps, however, it is imperative that this suggested reading list of military literature be just the foundation of the interests of the individual officer. Every officer should develop a core library of classics that will guide thought and serve as a reference. The purpose of this library is to see what the writer saw, to develop the ability to agree or disagree with the writer and-most importantly-to add to the ability to think, to observe and to write.

Formal education is not a prerequisite for writing ability and having something to say. What is required is an interest in development of the skills and of the surrounding world. A few simple rules are helpful:

* The more simply a thing is said, the more powerfully it influences those who read it.

* There is always one best word to convey a thought or feeling. The use of a weaker substitute will deprive the writing of force and impact.

* Economy of words strengthens the writing.

According to Carl Sandburg, adverbs are better tools than adjectives because they enhance the verb and are active. Adjectives simply load down the noun.

Verbs make language live. The verb is the operative word; it gives the sentence meaning. Strength in sentence structure comes from emphasis on the verb.

Vague terminology and phrases are twice cursed: first, by the writer who lacked the precision to say what was meant and second, by the reader who must waste time and effort trying to determine what the writer meant to say. It is easy to fall back on service jargon. This is both pretentious and a waste of time. "I did," "we went" and the like are all in the dictionary. Use them.

An outline is imperative. It may exist only in the mind of the writer, but it must exist. Each piece of writing must have three things: a beginning, a middle and an end. Writing is similar to a journey. The destination-the conclusion-must be known before the effort is begun.
One must write with the words that most accurately express his or her thoughts. The words must be understandable to the audience. Anything else misses the point.

Suggestions on writing could fill the remainder of this book. The important points are to master the language, practice the skills and have something to say.

Speaking

Words are the dress of thoughts which should no more be presented in ragged tatters than your person should.

-Lord Chesterfield

Being able to speak well is as important as being able to write well. For military officers, it may be even more important. Judgments formed by superiors and subordinates are based in large part on what an officer says and how it is said.

This is not a book on public speaking. Existing books present in much more detail the nuances that make an effective speaker. Besides, most new officers will not be required to make speeches to Super Bowl-sized crowds. They will be required, however, to present opinions, give briefings, talk to their people in both small and large groups and even represent their units or possibly their services.

Fortunately, most military audiences are sympathetic, even if they have to be there. They get restless, resentful and hostile only when the speaker is dull, attempts to impress them with a large vocabulary or talks to them as if they were candidates for graduation from the third grade. One key to being an effective speaker is to be interested in the topic. The interest will become obvious to the audience, and they will forgive minor stumbling. If they are talked to, not at, they also will forgive even obvious errors of syntax or pronunciation.

Sometimes it is helpful to use an attention-getter to start the speech or training session. The attention-getter must fit the audience. One of our most famous presidents opened a speech to the Daughters of the American Revolution with the line, "My fellow immigrants." He was right, of course, but was never invited to return to speak to the organization that admits only persons who can prove that an ancestor fought for independence.

One school of thought held that a presentation should be aimed at the upper 25 to 30 percent of an audience and that they would bring everyone else along. The people who did not understand would, as the logic went, be given something to which they could aspire. That logic may work well in a theological graduate seminar, but is out of place in a military setting. If, for example, everyone is to be on the parade ground at a specific time and in a specific uniform, everyone in the audience must understand what time and what uniform. This does not require words of one syllable. It does mean that one must know the group's ability to understand and must key the presentation accordingly.

Everyone loves examples. Humorous examples are even better received. The more times a speaker can drive home the point, the better it will be understood. A famous evangelist used an example to explain the slow growth of the early Christian church. He said, "It really should have grown faster. It would have except for Peter. As you read the Bible, do you notice that Peter was only half smart? He had to be, because the lord had to tell him everything three times!"

It may be coincidental, but all manuals about military teaching stress the "three times" approach. Tell them what you are going to say, say it, and then tell them what you said is the current logic. Studies show that the third time a person hears, sees or feels something, it has been learned. All the stories and anecdotes do is to let a speaker or instructor say the same thing in a slightly different way.

Humor is important, when it is appropriate. It provides counterpoint and spice to an otherwise serious profession. It is not easy to be funny. Otherwise, more of us would become professional comedians. Though not easy, it is not difficult to be humorous, and being humorous can help an officer become a good speaker. When John Paul Jones was under attack by the British and was asked to surrender, he responded, "I have not yet begun to fight." Not so often quoted is the reported response to this line by a Marine who was hanging from the rigging, blackened with powder and wounded in the leg. He shook his head in dismay and muttered, "Some guys never get the word!"

Humor has been defined as what happens to the other guy. It will not work if a speaker doesn't try to use it as part of his or her speaking ability. It will never work if it is racist, derogatory to anyone or makes light of the supposed qualities of any group of people. Ethnic jokes and stories have no place in the public presence of any officer.

The Armed Forces understand that people must develop the skills required for effective writing and speaking and will provide opportunities of increasing scope for the officer to develop them. Actual development is up to the officer.

The Art of Instruction

Keep it simple.
Have but one object at a time.
Stick to that object.
Remember that levity is not a sin.
Be enthusiastic.
Put out the ideas as if they were as interesting to you as to your
audience.

-Brig. Gen. S. L. A. Marshall

These simple rules will get an officer well on the way to becoming a good teacher. Great teachers are rare and well worth trying to find and learn from. As the poet Kahlil Gibran noted, "Wise indeed (is he) who does not bid you enter his house of wisdom, but rather leads you to the threshold of your own mind."

Teaching is the first and most important job of any officer. An officer will be either in school or training a replacement until the day after retirement. Retirement day normally is the last chance to pass on the wisdom and knowledge of a professional life. When that day comes, one of the last duties of the professional officer is to find a way to share the thoughts of an entire career with those to whom the service is being entrusted. It may be less eloquent than the carefully worded and classically presented phrases of a MacArthur or Eisenhower, but each retiring officer will have some thoughts worth sharing. If, as this book suggests, some of the career has been spent actually thinking about the service and trying to make that service to the nation meaningful, an officer cannot help having thoughts that, when articulated, will lead others to know and understand.

Showing others how to learn and understand for themselves is the essence of teaching. Instructing or being instructed is an essential duty of every officer, the newest 0-1 to the chairman of the Joint Chiefs of Staff. It may not be classroom instruction, but it will be teaching all the same.

Becoming a teacher requires knowing the subject, knowing people and

being able to communicate. All are equally important. Few, if any, subjects, once learned, do not result in some kind of behavior change. The
key is what sinks in and is retained.

A cynic of the personnel system used to give some sardonic advice to
all newly commissioned officers: "On the very first day at your new duty
station, find a way to hit the flagpole with your car. Every day after
that that you do not hit the flagpole, the entire base will be impressed
with how quickly you have managed to learn." It is a silly story, but it
makes several points. Everyone can learn. Some learn more quickly than
others. Example is one of the better teachers and a cornerstone of the
officer's life.

Socrates and Aristotle, two of the greatest teachers in recorded
history, used similar approaches to leading people to the light of
knowledge: example and question. They set the standards and were willing
to die to make sure the lesson was learned. They understood that people
learn for themselves and are not "taught." If the student can internalize
the information so that it makes sense to the student, then the instructor
has accomplished the goal. The student can "do" something he could not
"do" before.

In this regard, the Armed Forces have a very special role in the educational community. At one of the service academies, a department head
faced a problem. An instructor had taken up housekeeping with a woman
who worked in the department. She was married, but in the process of
divorce. The department head went to the legal office to find out if
there were any grounds to change the situation. He was given an emphatic
"no." He was told that he could not intrude on the off-duty time of the
officer. The officer's off-duty time was private.

The department head did not live in an ivory tower. He was well aware
of human frailty. He also was aware that the officer was an instructor
who taught both subject and by example. The officer's example was unacceptable. He summoned the officer and listed the options:

    a. Move out of the apartment,
    b. Find a way to marry the lady or
    c. Do neither-in which case, his usefulness as an instructor
    would be ended and he would be reassigned immediately.

The instructor ranted and raved. He was angered at the intrusion into
his personal life and felt that what he did on "his own time" was no one
else's business. The department head simply restated the options. They
resulted, he said, from the example the instructor was showing to the students. He gave the instructor the weekend to make a decision.

Do these situations hold any meaning for an Armed Forces officer?
They are relevant to the life of every officer. The first reality is that
everything an officer does is a lesson for everyone around him or her.
What is done, said or shown by example will influence both superior and
subordi-

nate. The second is that an officer does not have "own time," at least in
the sense that the instructor was using the phrase. An officer is an
officer 24 hours a day, seven days a week and 52 weeks a year and does not
have the luxury of self-indulgence or any other standard of conduct that
falls short of the ultimate in moral and ethical behavior.

The instructor spent the weekend in thought, which is the first requirement for any teacher. It is the time spent in self-instruction, research
and thought that leads to mastery of the subject and the ability to
present it well. The lector Primarius, or first teacher, of the Roman
Catholic order of Dominican priests always used the same opening in his
philosophy course for new seminarians. He would survey the class, who
waited with pen and paper at the ready, and ask, "What do you have in your
hand?" The answer invariably was either a pen or a pencil. "Philosophy
is about thinking. The pencil does not think. You think. So put down
the pencil and start using your brain."

Monday morning, the instructor moved to bachelor officer quarters,
announced his intention to marry the young lady as soon as it was legally
possible and returned to teaching.

In this day and age of marginal constraints on personal conduct and
the "right" to "do your own thing," how did the department head ever
succeed? By being right! It was Thomas Jefferson who put it best many
years ago: "In matters of principle, stand like a rock."

14

Communicating With Your People

One of the more difficult jobs for a newly commissioned officer is
that of counseling subordinates. When a subordinate has a problem, the
officer automatically is part of the problem. The officer may well be
younger than the subordinate but, as an officer, has a position to uphold.
If the subordinate reveals the whole truth, he may well be shooting himself in the foot. Most people have difficulty talking about themselves in
the first place and more difficulty admitting they have a problem.

Look at these considerations in reverse order. People find it hard to
talk about themselves only when the listener isn't obviously interested in
them. An officer who demonstrates real interest in people will find the
main problem is getting them to shut up. If the officer hides behind a
desk or hides behind limited time or hides behind giving orders and gets a
reputation for being unapproachable, it will not be the subordinates who
have problems, it will be the officer. He or she will be like the
commander at Camp Swampy-no one tells him anything.

Retired Army Gen. Alexander Haig put it simply: "A fundamental role
of leadership is communication."

Communication is, has been and always will be an almost magical process. To work, it needs two things: a communicator and a listener. Both
must use the same set of language parameters. Even non-language parameters must be understood by both parties. Hold up one finger in any bar
in America and the bartender will bring another drink. Doing the same
thing in Germany will get two drinks. What happened? References differ
from country to country.

In combat, it is imperative that all members of the unit-whether a
flight, a platoon or a flotilla-know exactly what is meant by each command or signal and respond accordingly. In aerial combat, the clock face
tells the direction of a threat. "Three o'clock high" means that an enemy
or unknown is approaching from the right and from above. In combat,
only the simplest directions have real value.

Good communication is essential to day-to-day operations and critical in increased readiness situations. A major problem is not the lack of communications, but the sheer volume of data that inundates all of us. Selecting the important data is a critical skill that all officers must develop. In an increasingly complex world that provides increasing masses of data, the ability to discriminate may be a determinant of an officer's success. Ability to determine what is important for the moment and for the future is hard-learned and requires practice. One of the most important elements of this discrimination ability is being able to keep the big picture in mind at all times. Discrimination is simple when faced with both a stomach ache and a fire in the house. The situation that requires immediate attention is known at once.

Rarely, if ever, will the choice be that simple. More often than not, the situation will have numerous inputs, a wide range of options and an equally wide range of results with which the officer must live. It is much like the cynical definition of an operational decision: a decision based on imperfect information, the result of which will end in life or death or no one caring in 30 minutes. It is the ability to be involved with, but not in, the situation that is important. It's a small but vital difference.

There are two basic kinds of communication in the Armed Forces. The first can be categorized as "keeping the troops informed." It includes the total flow of information, up and down the chain of command, that makes the system work. The second is the more personal communication involved in knowing and counseling people. Both involve some basic skills, and the first of these is the ability to listen. (There are people who are thinking what they will say next instead of listening to what is being said. They are one of life's most vexing irritants.)

It is imperative to hear what is being said, not what the listener wants to hear. To get this done requires paying attention to what is being said.

Equally important, the information must be presented as clearly and unequivocally as possible. "There are a whole bunch of tanks coming through the Fulda Gap" is about as useful as Uncle Harry's hat size. Facts, facts and more facts are the requirement.

Trust is imperative. To get people to go in a given direction and accomplish a common goal, they must believe they are being told the truth. It may be unpleasant truth, it may be incomplete, but they must have confidence that the communication is trustworthy. People willingly assume the worst in any situation where they think, or are told, they are not being kept informed. A paramount role of any leader is to "keep the troops informed."

A leader articulates the goals and makes sure that those goals are understood. A leader removes the mystery from the situation and provides the direction for all to follow. A leader provides the framework and makes sure that the who, what, where, when, why and how are fully understood by all. In Tom Clancy's book, The Hunt For Red October, the entire fictional plot of a submarine defection hinges on the reverse of this concept. The submarine commander can defect only because the military system of which he is a part makes it a point not to communicate with the troops. The theory was that they would just do their jobs and have no idea what was happening until the defection was complete. That may sound unthinkable in a society that takes some kind of perverse pride in the ability to "leak" information and has more investigative reporters than philosophers.

The point is not one of secrets or leaks or the correct time to release information. In our country, a person who is going to lead volunteers must be certain the troops know the risks, the reason and their specific responsibilities. They don't get a vote on the action. That issue was settled when they enlisted or took the oath of office. Still, they have a right to know all that can be told. They expect to hear it from their officers.

On a more mundane matter, heterosexuality and the avoidance of drug use are conditions of employment for Armed Forces members. There are no gray areas. The message is clearly provided to all. If caught violating either standard, the response is automatic and irrevocable. The issue is not whether that position is correct or incorrect. The reality is that the position exists and is understood by all.

There are some special problems inherent to the Armed Forces, problems that officers must face and work with their people to solve. In the most general sense, the problems deal with expectations. Expectations of the Armed Forces for the acceptable life-style, moral codes and behavior of their people are clear and well-taught. Less clear is how well these expectations match the expectations and accepted behavior norms of many of the people. In recent years, the services have begun to examine the disparity and to find ways to close the gap with programs to deal with spouse and child abuse and drug or alcohol abuse.

In counseling people, it is important to remember there is a wide range of specially trained people that the Armed Forces have available to assist with problems that are beyond the individual officer's ability to handle. Chaplains, lawyers, financial advisers and other specially trained professionals are available to help handle problems like spouse and child abuse, rape and drug and alcohol abuse. For simpler problems, the Red Cross is an effective tool to confirm the status of a particular problem.

A few broad, common-sense rules will enable any officer to be more effective in counseling:

* Privacy is requisite, and the interview should be conducted without interruptions.

* A listless manner spoils everything, diminishing the force of reason and discouraging confidence.

* To put the person immediately at ease by some personal gesture is more important than observing forms.

* Thereafter; the situation is best served by relaxation of bearing rather than by tension.

* Any excess of expression is a failing, and above all, it should be avoided by the person to whom another looks for guidance.

* Listen well! The problem is real to the person looking for help. Listening well will aid in getting to the basis of the problem more quickly.

* No counsel that lowers self-respect is any good. Moralizing and generalizing about the human failures that caused the counseling is a waste of time.

* Decisions that are wholly of the heart and not of the mind will ultimately do harm in both places.

* No person will talk freely and at length if met by silence. An intelligent question encourages frankness.

* When one person loses possession of himself, it is all the more reason that the other should tighten reserve.

* Affectation in manner gives lie to credibility.

* To express pity for anyone does little to restore him and enable him to raise himself above pity.

* When people are burdened by a personal problem that excludes everything else, they must be led to something else.

* People can be led and guided to sound judgments, but, in the final analysis, it is they-no one else-who implement the judgment that they have made.

Discipline

To bring men to the proper degree of subordination is not the work of a day, a month or a year.

-George Washington

Discipline is learning what to do, when to do it and in what manner it should be done. For the Armed Forces, discipline is the standard of personal deportment, work requirement, courtesy, appearance and ethical conduct that will enable all to perform the mission with optimum efficiency.

Discipline is essential to successful accomplishment of a military mission because each mission requires a team effort. When each individual performs as a part of the team, success becomes possible, even probable. That, in turn, means that each individual has trained himself to obey orders and regulations.

In a free society, the only valuable discipline is self-discipline. It cannot be made to work with a gun, whip or any set of laws. Meaningful discipline comes about only when service members obey the rules that govern their conduct because they know and accept the rules.

Discipline must have a purpose. It must serve a function or subfunction that makes sense and is understandable. Catch 22's entire theme is the insanity resulting from blind acceptance of idiotic rules.

The other side of that coin is that-to the extent permitted by security requirements-each individual needs to be informed of the purpose of his actions. In no other military force in the world is this such an important part of military training, discipline and operations.

Saluting is not some kind of hysterical aerobics practice that the military uses to increase physical fitness. It is a symbol, dating back to almost prehistory, originally to demonstrate (according to an international legend) that a hand does not hold a weapon. In modern times, it recognizes the worth of the individual being saluted. Symbols like a salute are not a burden or chore but a willing acceptance of the value of all members of the profession.

President Ronald Reagan had told of being ill at ease when saluted by members of the Armed Forces and not having a clear way to respond and show both his acceptance of the salute and his recognition of the worth of the individual service member. He asked a senior member of the Armed Forces if it would be correct to return the salute. The senior officer responded, "Who is going to argue with you, Mr. President?" So Mr. Reagan adopted the practice of returning all salutes.

Author Robert Heinlein noted that formal courtesy between husband and wife is more important than it is between strangers. While he is correct and may well have identified the balm that has saved many a marriage, formal courtesy also is a large part of discipline.

Societies can function only when most of the society understands and accepts the rules that make the society work. All societies have some method of removing from the society those few persons who will neither accept nor follow the rules. Methods vary. Some societies cut off body parts to try to teach the lesson; some lock the offender in cages; some try to re-educate the offenders and return them to the general society. A few either will not or cannot learn to obey the rules of the society. Given reasonable rules, well taught and germane to the situation, most people will learn and follow them.

Dictatorships and other repressive forms of government have few problems with order and discipline. They became what they are by controlling the "enforcers of discipline." These "enforcers" have used many names: Ton Ton Macoute, SAVAK, SS and the Secret Police are a few. Names are not important, and methods rarely vary. Those societies achieve discipline by generating fear, terror and instant retribution for any act considered "wrong" by the enforcers or those for whom they are acting.

Societies based on the dignity and worth of the individual have a much different set of discipline problems. The right to impose discipline is derived from the people and, if abused, will be withdrawn. Americans have seen fit to revoke even parts of the Constitution that did not meet the needs of the people. According to one student of government, "It may be easier to be a dictator than the elected leader of our nation."

A military system operating in a free society amends some basic rights of citizenship so that the system, with its demands and responsibilities, can function. A fundamental difference between the civil sector and the military was encapsulated by Rear Adm. Norman "Bulldog" Coleman: "There ain't no votes on a ship."

The American in uniform does not have the same latitude as a civilian in the exercise of rights. The most obvious difference is that the Armed Forces member does not have the privilege of quitting. If the member refuses to accept the demands of discipline, the Armed Forces must correct the behavior in a formal way.

Much has been written about the supposed demise of discipline in the latter stages of the Vietnam War. Cause of the deterioration has been placed largely at the feet of a permissive society. The feet do the walking-the head does the talking. Deterioration of discipline has one root cause. It always has been and always will be the same cause: lack of leadership. Leadership's very definition describes the problem. Leadership consists of achieving willing subordination of self to the demands of the mission. It is the leader who sets the standards of behavior and teaches the need to follow orders. When any mark of discipline is not being followed, the leader must look to himself for the cause.

It is naive to assume that all will willingly accept and adhere to Armed Forces discipline standards. Most troops, if well taught by example, will adhere to the standards. The level of discipline will be what the officers in charge choose to make it. That level should be the minimum necessary to get the best results from the majority. Discipline imposed to punish or appease either end of a unit population's bell curve usually has the opposite effect. Common sense is more useful than rigid adherence to rules and regulations.

Vice Adm. Ramsey worked the situation to achieve both discipline and morale. There is a limit to the number of people who can be absent from a ship at one time. Statistically, this number of people is always less than the number of port calls, emergency leaves and people whose wives are having babies. Adm. Ramsey put it on the line with his people: "If we maintain the standards of discipline and you prove to me that we can get the mission done with fewer people, I will authorize more people to take shore leave and to go home to be with the family for the birth of a child." Re maintains that it never failed to produce both exceptional discipline and special effort. The technicalities of strict adherence to regulations were less important than common-sense management. Re had created a team of willing, self-disciplined people.

As differences between peacetime and direct combat operations become less visible, the need for discipline becomes increasingly evident and important. The luxury of "forced marches to test mettle" has long since passed. Leadership develops the habits of discipline in peacetime. It instills the knowledge that the orders are right and the understanding that the leader's integrity is such that the orders need not be questioned. With such a basis, the demands of combat discipline can be achieved.

A wise, combat-seasoned veteran once said, "You cannot fool the troops! They know and will accept tough training. They will never accept Mickey Mouse stuff that common sense tells them is stupid or a waste of time."

If a purpose of discipline is to get people willingly to exercise the greatest freedom of thought while promoting the feeling of responsibility to the group, then, once it is achieved, the notion of failure is unlikely.

Reward and Punishment

One duty that falls directly to each officer is administering the system of rewards and punishment. Military life requires obedience to a complex set of rules and regulations. Violations of those codes cannot be tolerated without prejudice to the discipline of the entire unit. The commander or officer in charge is given considerable room for judgment in deciding whether the offense requires a court-martial or can be handled administratively within the unit.

The idea that military systems have the right to reward and punish is ancient. The right is questioned occasionally. Few persons question the right to reward, only the need to punish. With the blindfold on Lady Justice, the scale at times was unfairly tipped to one side or the other. Those occasions can affect morale, because good order and discipline exist only where all members of the organization believe that fairness or justice can be expected from those in charge.

Even the smallest child resents any perceived injustice. It may be punishment for an offense not committed or unavoidable. It may be partiality toward one or more siblings. But the offended child's resentment is unmistakable. The facial expression is eloquent, and sometimes there are wails of protest.

Our nation is based on law, and the military establishment has its own body of law. The Uniform Code of Military Justice provides one standard of treatment for all service members. It specifies the general nature of offenses against society and special offenses against the good order and discipline of the military service. Except for the more serious offenses, which by their nature also violate the civil code, it does not flatly prescribe trial and punishment. Military law, in this respect, has more latitude than civilian criminal law with regard to minor offenders. Rarely arbitrary in its workings, it presupposes the use of corrective good judgment at all times. Its major object is not the punishment of the wrongdoer but the protection of the interests of the dutiful.

This concept led various service secretaries to decide that court-Martial charges against certain ex-POWs, who on clear evidence had actively aided the enemy in North Vietnam, would be dropped. They had probably commited the alleged acts, but no greater good would have been served by a public trial. In all cases, the best policy is one that depends for its workings on the sense of duty of people toward each other, thereby strengthening that sense through its operation.

The other side of that coin was clearly shown during World War II in the handling of an American technical sergeant who had been discovered sabotaging his own squadron's aircraft. He had placed thermos bottles, filled with explosives and armed with altitude-sensitive fuses, in a key hatch on board the aircraft of his unit. He had destroyed 10 aircraft and killed more than 100 men before he was caught. Tried and convicted, he was sentenced to death by firing squad. After the commanding general's complete review of the case, the findings and the sentence, the appointed day arrived. The entire squadron was marched to the end of the runway, where the commander picked a firing squad composed of men equal in rank to the convicted service member, and the sentence was carried out on the spot. Why had this man become an active traitor? For less than $100 per person he killed!

The attitude of the Armed Forces toward correction as a means of promoting the general good also places a large trust in the justice and good will of the average officers. The assumption is that they will follow the advice of Ovid when he said, "let the ruler be slow to punish and swift to reward." The system teaches officers of all ranks that passing critical, impartial judgment on the conduct of those they lead is part of the job. This does not require a special wisdom that only a few can attain. The system works when the authority that has been given is exercised on those few who cannot, or will not, obey the rules.

At first glance, it may seem a heavy and difficult burden. It will never be simple and easy to judge individuals in relation to the affairs of an organization. With time and experience, the ability will become almost second nature. While never done without thought, it will be a part of an officer's skills.

First among the fundamental considerations that must be kept in mind for both reward and punishment is that rewards should be given to persons who deserve them. Undeserved rewards weaken the entire organization. Never pass up the opportunity to reward your people. The reward can be as informal as a pat on the back or as formal as a decoration. People will know when a reward is deserved and will never forgive or forget if some kind of recognition doesn't happen for a job well done.

The second consideration is equally simple. Punish those who deserve punishment. Equal and fairhanded punishment must be based on the individual's record and an understanding of punishment's purpose. Poor use of punishment is typified by the commander who was afraid to punish anyone and by his indecision punished everyone; the lieutenant who suffered such a bad conscience from his weak handling of a grave infraction that he threw the book at the next offender, thereby spoiling a good man and gaining the ill will of the company; the old-timer who smarted under excessive punishment for a trivial offense, broke under it, got into much worse trouble and became a felon; the fool who handled every case alike, instead of recognizing individual differences in human character; and the idiot who views giving punishment as validation of his position and rank. An officer can avoid becoming a part of the long and sorry list by following the "Golden Rule" policy toward subordinates.

If obedience is a moral quality, punishment should be employed as a moral act. The prime purpose of the act is to nourish and foster obedience. Unlike the Roman Praetorian officers who taught the legionnaires to wear their breastplates by the simple expedient of killing the first one who forgot to wear his, it is now necessary to think over, to compare and to weigh punishment's probable effects on the person being judged and on the system. The question is: "What good will be achieved?" If the answer is "none," punishment is not in order.

If punishment is necessary, however; the case must be handled in a prompt, positive manner that leaves no doubt the officer is certain about the judgment. People know when they are in the wrong and will have increased respect for the officer who knows what should be done and states it clearly. Reasoned firmness is the first step in the process. Waiving punishment is as foolish as threatening to punish and not following through. The officer who runs around threatening to court-martial his subordinates is simply announcing his own weakness.

To punish the group for offenses committed by two or three unidentified members of the group is no more acceptable in a military organization than in civilian society. It is a stupid practice that will forfeit the loyalty of the best in the organization.

Praise in public and punish in private is a good guide for any officer. Despite exceptions, the guide helps to get the point across. It avoids undermining the confidence of either superior or subordinate.

A basic duty of any officer is to intercede and protect subordinates from injustice. The duty is so basic that an officer must be willing to risk professional reputation when convinced that either higher authority or civil authority is acting unfairly. It is not an officer's duty to try to cheat the law or thwart justice, however, just because the accused is that officer's subordinate.

The best policy on punishment is to eliminate the frictions that cause most of the transgressions. People know when they are being treated fairly as individuals and as a group. They know when either reward or punishment is due. They expect their due. Duty is the sure proving ground. People should be judged on their all-around performance. It is the long haul that matters.

One last thought on the idea of reward and punishment: Just as the punishment must fit the crime, it is folly to give a reward that will prove expensive to the recipient.

This discussion of reward and punishment is no substitute for a working knowledge of the Uniform Code of Military Justice, the Manual for Courts Martial or the awards and decorations regulations of the particular service. The philosophy, however, is consistent with the spirit and intent of these documents. Understanding the philosophy is only half the job; the other half is study of the documents to actually know what they say and mean.

Morale

Morale is when your hands and feet keep working when your head says it can't be done.

- World War II Blue Jacket

Morale is when a soldier thinks that his army is the best in the world, his regiment is the best in the army, his company the best in the regiment, his squad the best in the company, and that he himself is the best damned soldier in the outfit.

-Maj. Gen. James Ulino

What makes people tempt the devil? What gives people the chutzpah to know that they "can?" It is morale. Morale is the quality that says "we can and we will." It is the mainspring that makes units work and work well. It is the opposite side of the discipline coin. Instilling both depends on the leadership's understanding of how they interact.

We have long since learned that the ideal of discipline is far more important than the pattern. The elder Moltke, one of the great masters of the military art, taught his troops the supreme importance of forming accurately in training, since the perfection of their formations would determine their efficiency in battle. Yet in the Franco-Prussian War, the formations proved utterly unsuitable to the theater's heavily wooded terrain, and new ones had to be devised on the spur of the moment. This lesson has been relearned in almost every war.

The keys to success in battle are adaptability to the situation and the understanding that the purpose of discipline is mutual support. Tactics must change to meet the situation, and patterns of operations may well change overnight to those that will work. When this happens, the only disciplinary residue that will matter is obedience to orders. It is neither the length of a stride nor the angle of a hand in a salute that measures discipline. The yardstick of discipline is the confidence in the judgment that the orders are being given for mutual support and for the greater good.

Confidence is the sine qua non of all useful military power. The moral strength of an organization's unity comes from the unit members' faith that they are being wisely directed and from the leadership's faith that the orders will be obeyed. When units are tempered by this spirit, there is no limit to what they can do. They become invincible. Without this confidence, any military body, even though forced to train using patterns of discipline, will deteriorate into rabble under the conditions of extraordinary stress of battle. Discipline's ultimate test is what happens when life is at stake. Do they stand or run? History has recorded countless examples of successful military forces that had almost no discipline when measured by the usual yardsticks, yet had a high battle morale that produced the ideal of discipline that defeats the enemy. The key is leadership.

If we accept the premise that discipline is not a ritual or a form but simply a course of conduct that is most likely to lead to the efficient performance of an assigned responsibility, then it follows that morale does not come from discipline, but discipline from morale.

Recruits are exposed to measures designed to instill discipline from the moment they take the oath. The first lesson is the necessity for obedience. Even before they learn to think as a group and before the attitudes of that group begin to affect them, they are being disciplined. It is a difficult time. Discipline bears down before morale has an opportunity to surface. It begins when the member starts thinking as part of the fighting establishment and no longer as a civilian. From that point on, everything that is done to nourish the military spirit and increase the thirst for professional knowledge is helping to build morale.

It takes just a short time to learn one's way around in the services. People quickly lose the initial fears and acquire both strength and wisdom from the group. They become able to evaluate both their own progress and the leadership of superiors in very clear terms. From this point on, discipline has little to do with the growth of morale. People either belong to and support the group or they remain outsiders forever. They are able to recognize discipline that is right and reasonable as being good. They also recognize almost instantly when it is either too harsh or too lax. The latter will ruin morale.

The individual, like the group, can be hurt by being pushed beyond sensible limits, but morale will suffer more if no real test is given to ability and moral powers. The greater the person's intelligence, the stronger the resentment. The enlightened mind always has the greatest measure of self-discipline. It also has a higher sense of justice, injustice and reasonable requirements of duty. People need productive and meaningful work challenges. They need to be proud of what they are doing. It is that simple.

Morale is a product of both the mind and the spirit. The question is how it is to be developed. It comes first from a sense of identity. It comes from the pride of belonging and doing worthwhile things. It comes from the confidence in the leaders and the respect that the leaders demonstrate for the value of the subordinate. It comes from the idea of meeting the challenge and winning.

During the battle at Khe San, a few Marines decided that they had had enough. They boarded a C-130 and ordered the aircrew to fly them to Da Nang. Few reasonable people will argue with armed, hostile Marines. The aircrew flew to Da Nang and radioed ahead that they had a problem.

Khe San was not a fun place. It was as difficult, bloody and rotten as any battle of the war. It was understandable-but not acceptable-that the pressures of the battle would make any sane human want to leave. History does not record the name of the Marine major who met that C-130. Dressed not in battle gear, but unarmed and in a simple duty uniform, he entered the aircraft through the rear entrance and walked to the middle of the cargo bay, where he was surrounded by the battle-weary Marines who had commandeered the aircraft. It could have been a dark day in military history; it could have been a violent confrontation.

Instead, the Marine major quietly, and with exceptional courage, told all the men: "You are United States Marines. That makes you special. Marines don't quit until the battle is over. We have a battle to fight at Khe San. Take your seats and get strapped in while I tell the aircrew to take all of us back to Khe San." They did, he did, and the rest is history.

The lesson is clear. One officer can accomplish an apparent miracle by an act of will and courage. Morale of force flows from the self-discipline of the leader, and in turn, the discipline of the force is re-established by the upsurge of its moral power.

It would be futile to comment on the nature of moral leadership were it not fully within the power of average young officers to become moral leaders. The art of leadership, the art of command, is the art of dealing with humanity, a humanity of potential, of dreams, visions and intelligence.

Diligence in the care of this humanity, administration of organizational matters with a consistent standard of justice, military bearing in one's self and the knowledge that military ideals are nourishing to both spirit and body are the four fundamentals a commander uses to build morale. There are other forces and mechanisms. Most of them come under the general heading of management and are discussed in other parts of this book.

Esprit

To better understand esprit and its role in building the Armed Forces, it is necessary to look beyond the organization and consider the people.

The lives of most people are organized around only a few basic loyalties. The degree of satisfaction they derive from existence usually can be measured in terms of service to those loyalties. The first loyalty is to self. Without it, all else is impossible. If people cannot acquit themselves well for their own sake, they cannot honor anything less personal. Along with loyalty to self comes loyalty to beliefs, family, country, friends and humanity in general.

Stated as a fact and not a concept, the interesting and important thing that happens when people enter the military service is that the moment they take the oath, loyalty to the nation becomes the first priority and ranks first on the list of obligations, duties and responsibilities. To get ahead and to serve themselves well, they must persevere in ways that are most useful to the nation, the service, the unit and themselves. They will not get rich serving the nation, but will be compensated well with honor. In this life, service to the nation is not an abstract notion. It is a daily act of service. Military people assume a new life and new friends.

In this radical reorientation of the individual life and the arbitrary imposition of a commanding loyalty, we find the key to the esprit in any military organization. Esprit is not something given to a unit in the past. Esprit is dynamic and vital-taught by older to newer members of a unit. Forget the idea that esprit is what the unit gives the person because of some spark of past glory, battle pennon or legendary exploit. It is what the unit gives the person in terms of spiritual force translated into constructive good. Considering what the unit has taken from them initially, its obligation is great indeed.

To see this clearly, we need to look once again at what happens to the individual when donning the uniform. Life is changed in broad fundamental ways. Legal status is changed; the extent and intensity of obligations are magnified. Individuals put aside the banner of individualism for that of obedience. Yet in the words of Charles Bernard, former president of the National Science Foundation, "Scarcely a man, I think, who has felt the annihilation of his personality in some organized system has not also felt that the same system belonged to him because of his free will to choose to make it so."

The thoughtful officer will remember that relationship and the time-proven words of Gen. James G. Harbord in The American Army in France. He said, "Discipline and morale influence the inarticulate vote that is constantly taken by masses of men when the order comes to move forward-a variant of the crowd psychology that inclines it to follow a leader. But the Army does not move forward until the motion is carried.

'Unanimous consent' only follows cooperation between the individual men in ranks."

He suggests that the multiplied individual acceptance of a command alone gives that command authority. It is no less true that the multiplied rejection of a command nullifies it. In other words, authority is more the creature than the creator of discipline and obedience. Authority relies more upon respect than respect is founded upon authority.

Esprit is the product of a thriving mutual confidence between the leader and the led; it is founded in the faith that together they possess a superior quality and capability. No record of past greatness can make people serve better, if they are being served badly. Unless the organization's past conveys to its officers a sense of being especially chosen-and unless they respond to this trust by developing the strongest sense of duty toward their subordinates-old battle records and past triumphs can be flushed down the drain, since they will not rally a single person in the hour of need.

Moral and Physical Welfare

Morals are a personal affair; in the war of righteousness every man
fights for his own .

-Robert Louis Stevenson

Morality, when vigorously alive, sees farther than intellect.

-J. A. Froude

The moral of this chapter is that when people are moral, the moral power that binds them together and fits them for action is given its main chance for success.

There should, therefore, be no confusion about how the word is being used. We are speaking both of training in morals for everyday living and of moral training that will harden the will of a fighting body. One moment's reflection will show why they need not be considered separately.

American Armed Forces' doctrine states that when people conduct lives built on high moral standards and physical fitness, they tend to develop qualities that produce inspired leadership and discipline. It is not a new notion; it can be found in any great military force in the past. It was not developed to gratify clergy or reassure parents. That is important, but the fundamental idea is that it works!

The doctrine comes from nation's experiences in war and what the Armed Forces learned by measuring their own services. Happily, the facts are consistent with a common-sense evaluation of the case.

Let's figure it out. The hedonist cry of "All things in excess! Moderation is for monks!" May work for the pleasure chasers, but not for the Armed Forces. To be temperate in all things, to be continent and to refrain from loose living of any sort are acts of will. They require selfdenial and forgoing what may be more momentarily attractive in favor of things that should be done. Some individuals are never tempted to digress morally, but the rest of us are all too human. What we renounce in the name of self-discipline, sometimes at the cost of considerable inner stress, we endeavor to compensate for by the gain in personal character. It isn't easy, but only the most cynical observers deny its worth.

The strength of will that enables a person to lead a clean life is no different from the strength of purpose that equips that person to follow a hard line of duty. They go hand in hand, and both are necessary. When strength of purpose or will fails, it is possible still to find first-class fighters, but not officers. Vices or weaknesses are not things to be proud of, but to be overcome. The nature of the beast is that we all have weaknesses or vices. It's called being human. As Seneca said about Hannibal, "He conquered by weapons, but was conquered by his vices."

The process that builds muscle also trains and alerts the mind. Every physical act must have as its origin a mental impulse, conscious or unconscious. Training people to master their muscles helps train them to master their brains. They come out of physical training better conditioned to meet the demands of the profession and better prepared to think about how and why they are moving, which is true mobility.

No matter how great the inertia, the boredom and the grumbling, it is not a kindness to seek anything less than maximum physical fitness. Part of an officer's job is to ensure that members of his or her command have every survival edge that can be provided. If people lack the coordinated response that comes only from long, varied and rigorous exercise, they will lack cohesion in action, have much higher combat losses and uselessly expend much of their initial velocity.

When training people, the point is to attain the best condition that each of them can achieve-not to demonstrate that an officer's personal limits equal that of a decathlon entrant. The point is conditioning, not proving that exhaustion hurts. For the officer who has not been an active athlete, the conditioning process will serve also to demonstrate that all of us have the ability to function in a demanding physical world. We can be better than we think we are. It is not superhuman effort that lets people stand watch after watch or pull seven G's in the bombing pattern or spend days searching for a lost civilian or make a forced march to a new position or endure the stress of an amphibious landing. It is the long and sometimes dreary process of physical conditioning to meet these demands that has made the difference.

The Armed Forces place great emphasis on team sports. It makes little difference whether the team member is officer or enlisted. The object is twofold: Encourage the idea of teamwork toward a common goal, and make the conditioning process less dreary and mechanical. While most competition is friendly, it reinforces the notion of "us" and "them" and esprit. The fate of the world probably will not be determined directly by the outcome of the All-European Football Championship, but the game does provide an exceptional vehicle for demonstrating the military mission of willing subordination of self for the common good. This time it is

football; the next could be Orenada, Lebanon, Libya or any trouble spot
to which duty calls.

The gain in moral force deriving from all forms of physical training is
an unconscious gain. Will power, determination, mental poise and muscle
control all march hand in hand with the general health and well-being of
the individual. Posture improvement and the rearrangement of excess
weight into muscles may require uniform alterations, but the end result
will be a more confident bearing that is so much a part of the perception
of leadership. The increase in physical capability to get the job done
also will increase the will to accomplish the job.

Any officer should recognize that while painstaking attention to the
physical welfare of the "troops" is both mandatory and common sense,
the thoughtful attention to the spiritual needs and moral needs is a
larger concern. With increased priority to these, the physical welfare is
far more likely to come along satisfactorily. Again, it is the officer
who must set the example.

20

Duty

-Adm. Lord Nelson, at the Battle of Trafalgar

*The two highest achievements of the human mind are the twin concepts of
'loyalty' and 'duty '. Whenever these twin concepts fall into disrepute-
get out of there fast! You might possibly save yourself but it is too
late to save that society. It is doomed.*

-Robert Heinlein, writing as Lazarus Long

Duty is a concept for action. It is repeated over and over in the literature and history of mankind. Roman matrons had one definition of
duty as they sent their young people off to war: "Come back with your
shield or on it!"

What does it really mean? It must be important, since all of the books
and teachings about Armed Forces officers stress the idea that duty is one
of the requisites for all members of the Armed Forces. It is called the
cornerstone of conduct and the framework of the system. But when stripped
of the platitudes and the philosophy, what does it really mean?

A very simple way to look at duty is to say that duty is doing what is
expected. For a fireman, it's putting out fires as well as possible. For
a mother, it's living up to the expectations of motherhood. In this
sense, doing one's duty or being a good person means living up to the
expectations of the individual.

Everyone has a responsibility to be a "good whatever." It goes with the
job as part of the job. It is inherent to the job or profession and
cannot be ignored. People can squirm like live worms on a hook, but the
facts will not change! The expectations for any job are well-defined by
the job, by the society and by the person who accepts the job. Legalisms,
or trying to use the idea of rights to avoid doing the duty called for,
are quite common and almost a habit for many people.

Rights are important. Rights also incur obligations. The first
obligation is to do the job to whatever standard is called for by the
society. If the

society is willing to accept and live with mediocrity, then it will be mediocre. It has defined the expectations for itself.

The Armed Forces lack the luxury of mediocre people, mediocre standards of duty and mediocre expectations. That concept was tried with Project 100,000, in which people who could not meet the entrance standards for the various services were still brought on board. The idea was that military service would achieve a miracle, overcome their educational or character deficiencies and lift the marginal people to the level of the qualified members of the Armed Forces. The result was predictable. The original entrance standards were correct, and those people did not fit the needs of the services. This project and others that attempted to use the Armed Forces as instruments for social change were soon abandoned.

It is difficult for many people to understand, but the purpose of the military is not the same as the purpose of social legislation or the purpose of educational programs or even the purpose of medicine. Those areas of life assume that it is possible to feed, educate or cure everyone. The Armed Forces start from the premise that sacrifice is part of the profession. However it is said, it comes back to this essential well for our type of democracy, but is the kiss of death in a military system. If no one has been taught the concepts of duty and ideals (or a higher call to action than that generated by pure materialistic considerations), the all-compelling unity necessary in the military system could not exist. In this light, duty and ideals are instruments of national survival for the military. They also serve to reinforce the spiritual fiber of the nation as people learn them and then return to the civil sector.

21

American Ideals

In a pragmatic sense, an officer's career will span that of at least four presidential administrations. Budgets will change, national priorities will run a spectrum, and those politicians who represent the nation will come and go as a reflection of that will. The economy will fluctuate, universities will open and close, and even religions will grow and shrink in emphasis and influence. Nations will come into being and disappear. In short, the business of the planet will continue its checkered progress.

The constant in this warp and weave will be the service officer, whose commitment to the Constitution, morals, ethics and the nation is the real shining light of liberty. It is the bedrock that will guarantee the freedom of the American people and the continuance of our nation.

The nation can accept nothing less. Armed Forces officers have no right to determine national policy. They must not, as has happened in our nation's history, distort information to serve the ends of anything other than the Constitution. Any such temptation must be ruthlessly controlled and stopped in its tracks.

The American military plays a special role in our nation. In one limited sense, it can be viewed as an instrument of national policy, that last bastion of diplomacy to be employed when the talking stops, the club that the politician wields to ensure that his point of view is the one that dominates the table of discussion, just as the legions of Rome or the hordes of Genghis Khan or the troops of Imperial Japan served the point of view of the leader.

The American military establishment will have a number of roles within any officer's lifetime. The officer may well be called upon to give life, fortune and sacred honor in defense of the nation. He or she will have to go through training that will teach the art of destruction of life and property and will be given chances to win the right to wear badges and ribbons that attest to prowess in these arts or in positions of great responsibility. The officer literally may be given the power to determine who Will live and who will die. He or she will be given great responsibility and authority in the name of your nation.

At the same time, the officer will be given the mandate to ensure that every action directly contributes to the defense of the Constitution and is legal and morally correct. That is the dichotomy that some can never understand. They see the destruction, but never the moral imperative. They can see only the similarities in the development of standards, training and armed forces. They cannot see, or choose not to see, that the fundamental purpose of the Armed Forces is totally different in free societies. They appear to be using Machiavelli as the principal philosopher for the control of people without reading all of the story and finding out that Machiavelli was perhaps the most unsuccessful military leader in history.

If people are to risk their lives, there must be a good, accepted reason, or they simply will not do it. People who are urged to sacrifice themselves and the future of their children for the notion that one end of an egg is better than the other will soon use on their leaders the business end of some instrument that terminates stupidity.

The problem with freedom is that once given, it becomes almost impossible to take away. Ours is a free society, and generation after generation of Americans has participated in the struggle to keep that freedom. It will always be in danger and must always be defended. Even today, in at least one city in America it is illegal to fly the national flag from city-owned buildings. In the very recent past, Americans have sold vital national secrets for the proverbial 30 pieces of silver. It would be all too easy to seek harsh and repressive "solutions" to these kinds of problems. That is not our way.

What other roles does the American military play in the defense of the Constitution? In one literal sense, the military is the very foundation for the continuance of the nation. In the military, the concept of civilian control of all aspects of national life is taught and upheld as a cornerstone of democracy. In the military, one out of every six members of the nation learns a trade or skill. In the military, the concepts of duty and discipline are taught and sustained.

The American military provides the nation with a repository for national honor, ethics and a way for young people to learn fundamental skills that will get them started as productive members of the nation. Remnants of racism, sexism and religious prejudice surface in the military from time to time. Sadly, these "anti-somethings" are reflections of society in general. Because the biases are so counterproductive and disruptive, the military has spent vast quantities of time and effort to counter and eliminate overt signs of bias.

One military role is to provide the nation with a single salad bowl, where young men and women from all parts of the nation, with all kinds of backgrounds and goals and motivations, can be taught common standards of language, ethics and behavior. Learning that there are things bigger than self is important for the nation. It is the exposure to the person who is "different" and the subsequent understanding that the "differences" are superficial that has helped the nation reduce prejudice. Each officer has a moral imperative to meet the standards of non-biased conduct and treatment of people.

When people are put in harm's way, there is no time to remember that Charlie is an "X" or Sally a "Y." It is important to know that Charlie and Sally are the best "Z's" available, the best "Z's" that can be molded. It is interesting to note that when people are treated as people, they display similar aspirations, fears and needs. We no longer conscript people into the military. Everyone wearing the uniform is doing so by choice. They are where they are because of a belief that what they are doing is going to be good for the nation and for themselves.

The 1922 Manual for Cadets at West Point devoted more space to the need to beat Navy in sports than it gave to the honor code. Cadets in all service academies have a time-honored tradition of seeing the other academies as the enemy. Nothing is inherently wrong with students being interested in student things. It is easier to identify with a specific unit or branch or service than with a nation. However correct and necessary it is to create a feeling of "us" and pride in unit or service, it is also correct and necessary always to keep in mind that the Armed Forces officer serves the nation, first, last and always.

The concept of unit or service is useful, but national goals, ideals and the totality of the Armed Forces are more important. The debate over roles and missions is just a debate whose end-purpose is the defense of the nation, not the size of the service budget or the right to be the sole possessor of information or equipment. It is as important as the debate over the structure of the Joint Chiefs of Staff.

The nation that places its future in the hands of a group of Armed Forces officers must also provide that group with both the tools and safeguards to make sure it can function as the nation's civilian leadership intended. The Armed Forces must be able to respond to the national demands for adequate defense in a balanced manner. They must serve the nation well, even if that means accepting personally unpalatable service mission changes.

Every Armed Forces officer must understand the national defense system and how it works. When an officer understands the national imperatives and his or her role in the defense of these imperatives, the nation can be secure in the knowledge that the trust given to its military officers is warranted. Only then can the nation be sure that legal exercise of authority and the determination of national policy will remain in lawful hands. Anything less is unacceptable.

22

You and Your People

Since much of this writing has focused on the interpersonal relationships of the officer as a leader, the purpose at hand is to cover certain
points not treated elsewhere. Within the military, simply getting along
with people is not enough. An officer's prime responsibility is to
develop people and make the most of their talents. The purpose is to make
a better and stronger military.

Nothing is more important. Mastering the skills and then doing the job
are cornerstones of a successful career. To get ahead, an officer must
understand what motivates people-individually and in groups-and must
understand the changes in motivation under varying conditions and various levels of stress or emotion. Books can provide only the index to the
understanding. The primary source of this learning is the observation of
people, the learning of what makes people tick.

The first step is to learn where the people came from-the "who they
are" and "what they are." They all have some basic things in common.
First, they are all volunteers. Second, they come from almost every seg-
ment of the society, with all of those segments' biases and perceptions.
Third, they all have certain expectations that they want the military to
help them fulfill. In short, they are not conscripts, and they are not to
be used as cannon fodder or bullet catchers. They may not have the same
background, mores or moral bases you have. Last, they all expect some-
thing-they may not be able to articulate it-from the military experience. They are the sons and daughters of the nation. They are entrusted
into the military's care, its training and its leadership. As a group,
they are no better and no worse than any in our nation: They are the
nation.

In an irreverent sense, they are like the "silly putty" used to make
images and things. What they become is a function of two things: the
military's leadership and their effort. Their effort alone is not enough.
Their forming must have guidance, direction, tempering and reward to
transform a malleable material into the tempered steel of individual self-

discipline and dedication to the unit, service and nation. They are humans with human needs, wants, desires, family relationships and occasional failures.

A new lieutenant, attending initial officer training, took a break between classes. Standing in the courtyard, he noticed that a group of initial enlisted trainees was also taking a break from classes in the same courtyard. As more people came out the respective classrooms, the two groups of people came closer together. The lieutenant waited and waited, but none of the new enlisted people took notice of his shiny new bars and none of them bothered to salute this paragon of officership. He walked up to the closest enlisted trainee, who greeted him with an all-American, "Hi, what's your name?"

The lieutenant was startled at this lack of respect for his office and person. "Do you see these?" he asked the recruit, pointing to the gold bars on his uniform. "Do you know what these mean?"

The recruit looked puzzled for a moment and glanced at the lieutenant's sleeve. Finding nothing on the sleeve, he smiled the happy smile of one whose problems are over. "Nope," he said happily. "You ain't got nothing on your sleeve, and my sergeant says that if you ain't got nothing on your sleeve, you ain't nothing."

Thomas Churchyard noted that "Sharp words make more wounds than a surgeon can heal." An officer who understands the job knows there is never any reason to use sarcasm, profanity or ad hominem arguments with anyone who doesn't get a fair chance to answer back. The object is to create a team, not enemies. An officer and his or her people are a team at all times, officially and socially. Good manners help to make the system work.

Names of people are important. The sweetest sound to anyone is his or her own name. Learn it and use it!

After a formal and impressive change-of-command parade and ceremony at Fort Carson, Cob., the departing battalion commander was honored at a reception at the unit recreation hall. As he greeted the line of soldiers, officers and their wives, he called each by name, asked something about their families or status and then greeted the next. The division commander watched from a nearby position with increasing interest. "He may well be the only battalion commander in the Army who can do that," the general said at last. "And I can guarantee you that not one member of his battalion will ever forget him, and many will seek to serve under him again."

Each service has individual perceptions and rules for social conduct. They are based on years of experience with the nuances of behavior that have proved workable for that service. Some are much more formal and restrictive than others. All are based on good manners, recognition of the worth of individual people and the enhancement of morale and esprit for that service. Learn the rules, follow them and enjoy them, because they are a part of your life as an Armed Forces officer.

All things in life that bring leaders pleasure do the same for their people. They have parents, spouses, birthdays, anniversaries, children, pro-
motions, illnesses, successes and failures. They respond to recognition
of these hallmarks in their lives. They are not meaningless ciphers, but
people who will only give their best when they get the best from their
officers.

That means that rank is most useful when it serves the needs of subordinates. Don't ask how the dining hall is doing. Visit it in the middle
of the night and find out. Don't ask the E-7 how people are doing in the
hospital. Visit them. When they come up with a good idea that works,
give them the credit. When they come up with one that doesn't or make
an honest mistake, remember President Harry S. Truman's sign on his
desk, "The Buck Stops Here." An officer gets paid to take the heat!

One last thought about an officer and his or her people: If the officer
is really doing the job, his or her people will be trying to do theirs.
When the officer has taught them well, he or she can give them a job and
let them do it. Supervise only enough to make sure that they don't need
your help to get the job done. Micromanagement will serve only to create
more supervisory work than any 10 people can accomplish.

Listening well may be an officer's most important skill.

The Code of Conduct

T he Code of Conduct is a living framework for all Americans. It
applies in both peace and war and is common to all Armed Forces. Much
like the Oath of Office, this simple declaration is part of the glue that
maintains the American military as a unique establishment subordinate to
civilian control. Some historical perspective of the code's development
is important, because it applies to all of the Armed Forces and must be
commonly taught, understood and applied.

It is easier to understand how the code applies in peacetime than war.
If you accept Air Force Gen. Curtis Lemay's dictum that there is no difference between the unlucky and the incompetent, then there are some
immediate problems in dealing with the issue of prisoners of war. President Richard Nixon put the clearest perspective on the POW issue. Simply stated, he noted that the nation must exert every effort to secure the
return of POWs, but that the fact of POWs could not dictate national
action in the conduct of hostilities. The issue is an emotional one that
requires thought.

In times past, people captured in battle had few options. They could
languish in prison until ransomed or the hostilities ceased, or they could
take up arms for the captor, or they could try to escape. Our nation has
used, until the post-Korean timeframe, many approaches to the issue of
captured Americans. During the effort to end domination of the central
Mediterranean by the Tripoli pirates, we ransomed some captives until it
became too expensive. Finally, an exasperated American president sent
Stephen Decatur to force an end to this intolerable situation. Much
later, we gave money to aircrews so that they could finance their own
escape or evasion. In a more recent war, we sent agents into hostile
territory with money to ransom captured American service personnel.

Over time, we developed a general concept that the captured American
was to give only name, rank, service number and date of birth; to escape

when possible; and to continue to be a member of the fighting force. Mechanically, the captured American was considered a combat loss, and in most cases the records of that American were sent to a repository until after the conflict.

Air Force Capt. Lance Sijan earned the Medal of Honor adhering to these principles until his death in the prison camps of North Vietnam. The case of an aviator in World War II was different. As a second lieutenant, he was shot down by the Japanese, but evaded capture. Shot down again within a month, he managed to escape from the prison camp and return to his unit. Strict American policy dictated that he could not again be sent into combat against Japan after his escape, because he would have been marked for instant death if captured again. The lieutenant was transferred to the European Theater and assigned to fighter-escort and ground-attack duty.

His aggressive, independent attacks on enemy ground forces gained a lot of attention. On a mission in northern Italy, he was again shot down. For many months, he evaded capture and attempted to get through to the American side of the lines. Getting through the enemy lines was not that much of a problem, but he could not penetrate the American lines.

After months of being passed from farmhouse to farmhouse and village to village, he finally persuaded some fishermen to take him out to sea and outflank the enemy lines. He was put into a small dory some distance at sea; he rowed himself ashore.

After some difficulty identifying himself as an American pilot, he was taken to Caserta, the headquarters of the Mediterranean Allied Air Forces. There, he was taken to the office of Gen. Ira Faker, where he reported for duty.

Along with being somewhat of a hero, he also presented a bit of problem for Gen. Faker. Through all of his combat, escapes and evasions and survival, his records had never caught up with him. He was still a second lieutenant. Gen. Faker said that any officer who had shown such dedication to duty was not going home with the same rank he had when he left the States. The general, who did not usually use an aide, made him an aide de camp long enough to promote him.

The Korean War produced many tales of heroism and even more unfounded rumors of dereliction of duty. Some rumors were based on fact. The enemy was using a technique that had been dormant since the Middle Ages, when captives were given a choice of death or fighting for the captor. They were brainwashing prisoners. They were making a clear, positive attempt to convert captured forces to the ideological precepts of the captor. This technique worked on a few prisoners, and they formally renounced the very ideals for which they had been fighting. The number, however, was much smaller than some critics of the day thought it to be.

An extensive body of literature examines this phenomenon from a hundred different points of view. The key factor among the victims of brainwashing was that, for some reason, they lacked a firm understanding of just what they were fighting for and what they were supposed to do if taken prisoner. Surprisingly, of the 7,190 U.S. prisoners captured by the North Korean and Chinese forces, only one officer was ever convicted for collaboration with the enemy.

One of the military's great virtues is the ability to recognize that perfection is an ideal that people need help in attaining. One solution was to provide a formal outline of conduct and behavior.

The outline has become the Code of Conduct.

Code of Conduct

1. I am an American, fighting in the forces which guard my country and our way of life. I am prepared to give my life in their defense.

2. I will never surrender of my own free will. If in command, I will never surrender the members of my command while they still have the means to resist.

3. If I am captured, I will continue to resist by all means available. I will make every effort to escape and aid others to escape. I will accept neither parole nor special favors from the enemy.

4. If I become a prisoner of war, I will keep faith with my fellow prisoners. I will give no information or take part in any action which might be harmful to my comrades. If I am senior, I will take command. If not, I will obey the lawful orders of those appointed over me, and will back them up in every way.

5. When questioned, should I become a prisoner of war, I am required to give only name, rank, service number, and date of birth. I will evade answering further questions to the utmost of my ability. I will make no oral or written statements disloyal to my country and its allies or harmful to their cause.

6. I will never forget that I am an American, fighting for freedom, responsible for my actions, and dedicated to the principles which made my country free. I will trust in my God and in the United States of America.

In an interview after being released from the prisons of North Vietnam, Air Force Col. William J. Baugh was questioned about being a prisoner and asked if he held any resentment toward Americans who protested U.S. involvement in Vietnam. His reply represents a clear statement of what the code is all about:

"I didn't enjoy the time in prison, the torture or the degradation. With very rare exceptions, anyone can be broken in body with enough torture. But the body will mend, and no one can change a mind with torture. The

Code of Conduct was the guideline that made the suffering bearable.

"We were hounded daily with publicity that condemned the war; movies, tape recordings, pictures and magazines that showed the depth of national concern about the conduct and fact of the war. We were even shown members of Congress and film personalities in situations that were ill-advised and perhaps even technical treason.

"The prison camp staff never understood why all of this information never changed most of our minds. What they really never understood was that the right of my people to dissent was the reason that I was in the prison camp. It was that right that I had been fighting for; and the fact of being in prison did not change my mind about that.

"I can't even really complain about being in prison. I knew it was a possibility when I stuck up my hand and took my Oath of Office."

Col. Baugh later was honorably retired with severe physical disabilities as a result of his ordeal.

Americans in Combat

NOTE: This chapter relates most directly to ground forces. However; the principles developed by Brig. Gen. S. L. A. Marshall included in the 1950 and subsequent editions are worth learning by any Armed Forces officer.

It is possible that the nature of war was changed over a small valley in southern Japan in 1945. From that time to this, it has become possible for the future of mankind to be changed with the press of a button and the delivery of a nuclear weapon to its target.

One consequence of this change may not be understood by members of prior generations. There will never again be a buildup period; there will be no massive troop movement by air or sea, no intelligence gathering that could lead to things like the "man who never was" and no Enigma or Ultra that could break the codes of enemies and lead to success in battles on the soil of countries whose names we can barely spell.

The changing nature of war means that the Armed Forces officer will face extraordinary challenges. First is that what used to be "peacetime duty" is now part of the nation's first line of defense.

The possibility of immediate combat dispenses with a buildup period. Current thinking is that our state of readiness precludes the enemy from attacking. In short, it is our ability to be prepared to enter combat that keeps the enemy from starting a global war. If we are to maintain the deterrent capability to preclude or to fight a global war and, at the same time, respond to levels of conflict short of global war, all military officers must understand the nature of American fighting forces when in combat of any kind.

Command and control of forces in combat can be mastered without experiencing actual combat.

For an officer who has made the most of the available training, it is not only possible but probable that the first combat experience will see the officer in full possession of the faculties and instincts necessary for both command and survival.

Practice and training in maneuvering forces is only an introduction to the educational process that makes this ability possible. A requirement for this ability is the continuing study of, first, the nature of man; second, the techniques used to produce unified action; and last, the reports of past operations and future options, which are all well-covered in the literature of the military profession.

If this collateral study is actively pursued by each officer, most of What has been learned during the training periods will become directly applicable to the actions taken and the ability to lead others when under fire.

Each service has its separate character and a fighting problem differing in some way from those of the other services. It is natural that the task of successfully leading forces in battle will be partly conditioned by the unique character and mission of each service. The differences in character and mission make it impossible and even foolish to impose a general doctrine on all American forces in combat, no matter what service or element to which they are assigned.

There are, however, a few simple, fundamental propositions that all Armed Forces officers can use to determine what they can expect from average Americans under battle conditions. Generally speaking, these propositions or expectations have held true for America's fighting forces from Lexington in 1775 to the present. They are fundamental to the way all American fighting establishments have built their discipline, training, code of conduct and public policy about the command of Americans in combat. Their premise is that successful application of these propositions in the past makes them valid for the future and will enable us to continue our traditions of freedom and individual dignity. These propositions are:

1. When led with courage and intelligence, Americans will fight as willingly and as efficiently as any fighter in history.
2. American keenness and endurance in war will be in direct relationship to the zeal and inspiration of the leadership shown.
3. Americans are resourceful and imaginative, and the best results will always happen when they are encouraged to use their brains along with their spirit.
4. Under combat conditions, Americans will reserve their greatest loyalty for the officer who is the most resourceful in the tactical employment of forces and who is the most careful to avoid unnecessary losses.
5. We are, to a certain extent, overreliant on machines because the nature of our civilization has made us so. In an emergency, we tend to look around for a machine or some other gadget that will make the job easier, instead of thinking about using our muscle-power to get the desired end. In combat, this is a weakness that can thwart contact and limit communication. Therefore, it needs to be anticipated and guarded against.

6. War requires neither the brutalization nor abuse of the American
    fighter. The need is for an alert mind and strong body. Hate and
    bloodlust are not part of the attributes of sound training under our
    American system. To clearly develop a line of duty, it is sufficient
    to point Americans toward the doing of it.

7. There is no such thing as an American fighting "type." Our best
    fighting men come in all colors, shapes and sizes. They come from
    every segment of society and section of our nation.

8. Americans in any group or unit assume that the officer leadership
    will be sound. They can be depended upon to fight loyally and obe-
    diently and will give a good account of themselves.

9. In battle, Americans do not tend to fluctuate between emotional
    extremes, in complete dejection one day and in exultation the next,
    according to changes in the situation. They continue, for the most
    part, on a fairly even keel, when the going is tough as well as when
    things are breaking their way. Even when heavily shocked by battle
    losses, they tend to bounce back quickly. Although naturally opti-
    mistic, they gripe and will react unfavorably to any officer who is
    always pessimistic and can only see the dark side of the situation.

10. During battle, American officers are not expected either to drive
    their troops or to be forever in the lead, as if praying to be shot.
    So long as the officer takes the same chances and shows a firm grasp
    of the situation and what needs to be done, the troops will go for-
    ward.

11. In any situation of extreme pressure or moral exhaustion where the
    men cannot be otherwise rallied and led forward, officers are ex-
    pected to do the actual physical act of leading both in person and
    by example, even if this means taking over what would normally be
    a subordinate's or enlisted soldier's role.

12. Most Americans are normally gregarious and are not at their best
    when required to function alone or in tactical isolation in battle.
    They are not kamikaze types or one-man torpedo types. As a result,
    the best tactical results come from situations and methods that link
    the power of one man with another. People who are new to units
    and have been carelessly received and indifferently handled will
    rarely, if ever; fight as strongly and as courageously as the
    newcomer who is treated with common decency, welcome and
    respect.

13. Within our school of military thought, higher authority does not
    consider itself infallible. Either in combat or out, any time a
    situation arises where a majority of military-trained Americans become

undutiful, that is a very good reason for higher authority to resurvey its own judgments, disciplines and line of action.

14. There is never a good reason to lie to American forces to cover up a blunder in combat. They understand combat and have an uncanny ability to find out the truth about tactical blunders. They will understand mistakes, but they will never forgive being lied to about them.

15. When spit and polish become so important that they seem to become the primary mission and the ranks cannot see any legitimate connection between these requirements and the development of an attitude that will serve a clear fighting purpose, it is time to question whether the emphasis on spit and polish is serving any good purpose whatever.

16. On the other hand, because the standards of discipline and military courtesy are designed for the express purpose of furthering control under the extraordinary frictions and pressures of the battle situation, maintenance of these standards under combat situations is as necessary as during training. Smartness and respect are the marks of military alertness, no matter how trying the situation. However, courtesy starts at the top with all ranks, and a decent regard must be maintained for the loyalty, intelligence and human dignity of all of the American fighting forces.

17. Even though most Americans enjoy a good standard of living in comparison to much of the world, in war they do not have to be pampered, spoon-fed and provided with every comfort to keep them fighting and devoted. They are, by nature, rugged and will respond to the most rugged conditions in a magnificent manner. Soft handling will soften the best of people. However, if moved by leadership that makes the best of a bad situation, even weak people can develop confidence and vigor in the face of necessary hardship.

18. Part of the American nature is to be careless with resources. This tendency follows Americans into the military service and, unless carefully regulated, can lead to difficulties in combat when the conservation of resources is necessarily an important part of combat planning. It is imperative and a primary job of all officers to ensure that the American fighting forces have the necessary tools to fight and that these tools be used in the most efficient way.

19. It is critical that combat troops be as physically fresh and mentally alert as is possible at all times. Extra work, exercises and any activity that does not directly support this goal is unjustified and unacceptable. Tired troops are half-whipped before the battle begins. Worn-out officers cannot make clear decisions. It is the conserva-

tion of energy, not the exhaustion of energy, that leads to successful operations.

20. In combat, it is vital that every member of the fighting force have the equipment necessary for the fight and not an ounce more. Extra weight or extra equipment can only detract from the capability to effectively wage the battle. Prudence is mandatory, but overcaution and overloading for all possible contingencies can destroy effectiveness and the ability to rapidly respond to changing battle conditions.

21. When engaging the enemy, one of the most important tasks of the junior field officers is to make sure that all of the fighting force is firing at the enemy. Even training and long practice in weapons handling will not ensure that the majority of the fighting force will actually fire at the enemy. One tenet of our American culture is that taking human life is inherently wrong. This is a deep-rooted emotion that is difficult to shake. It becomes less difficult to overcome as members of the fighting force realize that the enemy is actually shooting at them. However; during the initial stages of any engagement, it is most important that the junior leaders make sure that all members of the fighting force are firing at the enemy. This will require personal and intelligent direction of the individual fighter so that the response to enemy fire becomes an instinctive process.

22. Every member of the fighting force must be provided with the information necessary to ensure unity of purpose and action. No matter what service, it is critical that the fighting force understand the specific role and mission that it must play to ensure success. Because all battle plans will change to meet the changing battle circumstances, it is not necessary that everyone know everything. Even if the grand object may require apparently conflicting ideas and knowledge of these ideas may not be appropriate for all levels of the fighting force, it is imperative that every member of the fighting force be fully aware of the specific immediate steps that they are being required to accomplish.

23. Everyone gets scared in battle. Being scared is not an excuse for cowardice of any kind. The task of leadership is to stop cowardice by any means available that will not make matters worse.

24. The Armed Forces know that there are some individuals who cannot handle the stress and demands of combat, no matter how hard they might try to do so. It has nothing to do with loyalty or effort or willing spirit. It has to do with individual makeup and the ability of the flesh to respond to the demands of combat. If any individual has consistently demonstrated good faith and good intentions, then it is not cruel but also ignorant of the nature of man to punish,

degrade or humiliate such a failing of the flesh. This individual deserves the benefit of the doubt and a possible second chance. If, however, the past performance of any individual indicates that this kind of conduct is normal for the individual, then failure to take prompt action against the individual can only result in a degradation of the meaning of the efforts of the majority who are trying to do their duty.

25. The United States abides by the laws of war. Its Armed Forces are expected to comply with both the spirit and intent of these laws in all of their actions. The officers of the Armed Forces are the main safeguard to ensure that all members of the Armed Forces comply with these laws in both peace and war. It is only this respect for, and obedience to, the reign of law that differentiates American Armed Forces from wanton hordes of looters, destroyers of life and property and other immoral persons. Nevertheless, the very nature of war can lead some of the fighting forces to fall prey to violence and disorder and to participate in unlawful actions. These actions, at whatever level and for whatever reason, cannot be permitted to exist or continue. Only when all members of the fighting forces understand that every member of the fighting forces must be absolutely opposed to any unlawful conduct and that any such conduct will be met with immediate action will the United States be living up to its national goals. For the officer who either accepts an unlawful order or permits unlawful action by any member of his organization, it is no different than if he had committed the act himself.

26. One purpose of training is to get trainees to "open up" and share common goals and ideas. This can happen only in an atmosphere that encourages communication and thoughtful discussion and collective action. When people are afraid, they go silent, and this very silence intensifies the fear. In war, it is vital that communication continue and the fighting forces share each other's thoughts openly so they can strengthen each other and meet the mission demands.

27. Inspection is more important in the face of the enemy than during training, because a fouled piece may mean a lost battle, an overlooked sick man may infect a fortress, and a mislaid message can cost a war. By virtue of position, every junior leader is an inspector and has the obligation to make certain that the force is, at all times, ready and able to accomplish the mission.

28. In battle crisis, a majority of Americans present will respond to any person who has the will and the brains to give them a clear, intelligent order. They will follow the lowest-ranking man present if he obviously knows what he is doing and is the moral master of the situation.

29. Americans are uncommonly careless about security when in the combat field. They have always been so; it is part of their nature. Operations analysts have reckoned that this fault in itself can account for approximately one-third of our casualties. This weakness being chronic, there is no safeguard against it except supervigilance on the part of officers, and the habit is formed easiest by giving foremost attention to the problem during training exercises.

30. For all officers, it is just as important to understand the character of our fighting forces as it is to continue to study just how this character can be applied to all aspects of our training so that we can continue to strengthen each of our services. That armed force is nearest perfect that holds itself, at all times and at all levels, in the state of capability necessary to meet its specific mission in the defense of the nation and its Constitution. Only in this way can the concept of "officership" reach its full potential.

Present and Future Trends

Today's Armed Forces officer serves in a high-technology environment, using equipment that earlier generations only dreamed about to achieve mastery of a "battlefield" that may extend over great distances or may be confined to a very local area.

During World War 1(1914-1918), an infantry soldier could advance over terrain clear of enemy forces at about 2.5 miles per hour. In Vietnam, during the 1960s and 1970s, infantry units moved by helicopter at 150 miles per hour.

Reconnaissance of enemy forces moved within just a few generations from binoculars to hot-air balloons to aircraft of increasing complexity and capabilities. The next logical steps were reconnaissance by unmanned, remote-controlled aircraft and by satellites orbiting Earth. Both carry sensors and transmitters that enable commanders to keep watch over enemy movements and equipment in real time.

That kind of watch is essential to the modern commander. When the Italian fleet surrendered to the Allies in the summer of 1943, the admiral in command as it arrived in North Africa complained, "I have not been able to get steam up in a destroyer without you knowing about it, sometimes before I got the report from the ship myself!" An aerial-reconnaissance watch had been maintained for months. In the Cuba missile crisis of 1962, American photographs and electronic surveillance monitored each development of the missile bases and the arrival of the missiles. Other sophisticated systems told the Pentagon when the war-threatening nuclear warheads were dispatched toward Cuba. The information allowed the American military leaders and President John F. Kennedy to make vital decisions and take effective action to avert a grave threat to the nation.

During the 1982 war between Britain and Argentina, Soviet satellites kept watch over British fleet movements. The information they gained was passed quickly to the Argentine forces and undoubtedly affected some operations during the war.

Space is a military environment today. Thus the joint U.S.-Canada North American Aerospace Defense Command (NORAD) maintains a 24-hour watch on all objects orbiting the earth and even those that achieve only a partial orbit. In addition, the complex inside Cheyenne Mountain, at Colorado Springs, Cob., keeps track of "space junk." It is bits and pieces of satellites that deteriorated and returned to the deeper atmosphere, where the bulk of the equipment burned up on re-entry. It may be an apocryphal tale of the trade, but some Cheyenne Mountain veterans insist that they once kept track of a glove lost by an astronaut or cosmonaut.

Today's surveillance must be even more complex and complete than those that tracked the Italian fleet or Cuba missile sites. Whether a technical expert overseeing the operation of sophisticated systems or a commander or operations officer with broader responsibilities, the Armed Forces officer is a combination manager and leader with unique authority and burdens. Accurate, timely information enables the officer in charge to avert or deflect actions that would result in serious harm to the national interest or affect operations on a more local scale. The officer must be prepared to deal with such responsibilities.

Each officer in the chain of command must know the capabilities and limitations of the complicated systems available to carry out the mission. No one can be expert in all technical disciplines required by modern armed forces. More and more, though, each officer is likely to be a true expert in at least certain phases of the systems in use. The officer is likely to know how they interact with other systems to make up a complete defense.

All military equipment has been affected to some degree by advances in technology, but not all items have been changed radically. Electronics is an exception.

Development of the electronic microchip made it possible to miniaturize items of equipment that once required large power sources and, in some cases, substantial transport facilities. As a result, the individual in combat often is carrying sophisticated tools that greatly increase individual effectiveness. Some such gear is personal equipment; most is installed in aircraft, tanks, ships or mobile forward ground positions.

Introduction of the Airborne Warning and Control System (AWACS) was a marked step forward in combat management. Earlier aircraft-based systems had presaged the use of airborne command posts in which the combat director could see the entire field of combat, covering an area of hundreds of square miles, in real time. When members of the U.S. Joint Chiefs of Staff actually experienced the new capability of this equipment, they became enthusiasts for its purchase and deployment. Said Gen. David C. Jones, then chief of staff of the Air Force, "We flew well inside the Western side of the 'Iron Curtain' border and watched planes take off and land at Berlin's airports. Then when the range was reset, we watched the same thing going on at Warsaw!" That kind of technical marvel changes the whole concept of battle management for both airborne and surface combatants.

Modern battle communications systems give the individual soldier, Marine, sailor, airman or Coast Guardsman a satellite-based connection with his superiors and confederates and can tell him exactly where he is on the face of the Earth, within a few meters.

Modern Navy innovations include the semi-submersible heavy-lift ship, used to move smaller vessels over great distances of open ocean-the first was leased from Norway-and the high-tech Aegis cruiser, the most sophisticated combat control center ever put to sea. A leased squadron of Israeli fighters (F-21A Kfirs) became "adversary" aircraft for naval aviation training.

A spinoff of the new technology is an entirely new set of acronyms, initials and words in the military lexicon. An officer must know the new terms to supervise personnel to whom such language is second nature.

An example of the sometimes baffling habit of modern technical experts to talk in acronyms and abbreviations occurred when the U.S. Air Force chief of staff was addressing cadets at the Air Force Academy in Colorado. A first-year cadet was assiduously taking notes, but seemed baffled by a term the general was using repeatedly in the speech. Finally, the puzzled cadet leaned over to the officer seated at his side and whispered: "Sir, how do you spell 'seek-you-bye?' " The term for command, control, communications and intelligence (C31) is so often abbreviated that military personnel routinely had fallen into the habit of pronouncing the abbreviation as "C-cube, I."

Operation of today's equipment requires the officer to be physically and mentally fit at all times. While these are historical requisites of leadership in military forces, today no leader at any level can afford to sulk in the tent for days while deciding on a course of action. Vital decisions and action are required on the basis of combat information that tolerates no delay due to the temporary incapacity of the officer in charge. Substance abuse-the modern euphemism for abuse of drugs and alcohol-is unacceptable. The officer, whatever his rank or whatever level of responsibility, must avoid such personal abuses and must learn to spot abusers among subordinates and have the courage to correct the situation.

Perhaps today's greatest threat to military discipline, readiness and effectiveness comes from the abuse of drugs. It seriously threatens an armed force's ability to respond effectively to a crisis. Some governments that are known to sponsor international terrorism or guerrilla forces bent on the disruption of neighbor nations illicitly export illegal drugs as weapons of irregular warfare.

Each officer, therefore, must be vigilant in efforts to keep drugs out of

the command. Drug abuse is as old as society; that makes it no less
threatening to today's armed forces.

 Deployments of American forces around the world offer cultural, social
and educational opportunities for American service personnel of all
ranks. Their dependents, however, may find that local situations vary
both in the facilities available and the warmth of welcome Americans re-
ceive. In many areas, the local populace and government greet the Americans as friends, there to offer protection through mutual defense-
services. In others, the attitude may be cool or even openly hostile.
Any hostility is apt to come from a loud minority opposed not only to the
American presence, but to the purposes of the alliance that brings it.

 American families stationed abroad seldom consider that they could
become targets of kidnappers or other terrorists, but even individual soldiers have been taken in the post-World War II environment. Just as the
airman or soldier in aerial combat for the first time is surprised to
realize that the foe is aiming deadly weapons directly and personally at
him, the American abroad is slow to realize that the individual American
can be hated and harmed. Yet, during the period between the end of World
War II in Europe and the end of the Berlin blockade (and airlift) of
1948-1949, several hundred individual American soldiers were spirited
across the borders in and around Berlin by faceless foes. Not all were
recovered. The practice ended only when Army Gen. Lucius D. Clay,
American forces commander-in-chief in Europe, made it clear that effective retaliation would result if any more Americans disappeared in such
kidnappings.

 Terrorism, a new kind of warfare, attempts to elude responsibility for
hostile actions while exerting maximum pressure on the target nation or
people. While there can be no fixed plan of response to such clearly
flexible plans of attack, each officer must be aware of the threat and
ensure that command personnel are equally prepared to take precautions and
deter attack, but not degrade the mission.

 The Armed Forces officer must be aware of the family-group pressures
that can result from such alien situations. A highly trained and
motivated sergeant may be only marginally effective if forced to worry
constantly about the situation affecting dependents living outside
American jurisdiction. A knowledge of the appropriate Status of Forces
Agreement is an important management tool.

 The officer must know the situation of each family living "on the
economy" outside the base facility. Housing may be far below acceptable
standards. The idea of one washer and dryer for 24 families is repugnant,
yet it has been imposed on American service families in Europe and Asia.
The officer expected to lead the heads of those families in combat cannot
ignore such situations.

 Expenses in overseas assignments sometimes outrun incomes for those
in the lower ranks. A good officer must know what resources are avail-

able to assist those who may be in real financial distress. The officer also should be aware of reassignment procedures to be used when a transfer is the only way to retain experienced career people in service.

As in all assignments, there is no substitute for knowing the people and their problems as well as their capabilities.

Dealing with subordinates also means knowing how well-informed they are on the nature of the threats they face and how they react to those threats. The danger from nuclear weapons is constant in today's world. Proliferation of the number of nations possessing them is one of the primary worries affecting all governments. It is the subject of international agreements and talks.

Nuclear weapons are like the genie that could not be put back into the bottle. They have been invented, and a number of nations know how to make them. A somewhat smaller number of nations can manufacture and deploy them. Whether they have done so is, in each case, a major national policy matter.

Nuclear threats are a constant concern to Armed Forces families. A good officer must deal with fears to ensure that they remain in proper perspective, that they are not allowed to become a morale problem for the whole command and that both military personnel and dependents realize that whatever level of threat they face is probably shared by the local population.

Another threat that requires attention comes from the nature of potential enemies of our country. Each officer has a leadership obligation to inform command members of the threat's nature, its history, its capabilities and what it has meant to other nations that have fallen to its actions.

In our day, the threat of international communist forces, whether the movements of national forces by communist nations or the use of proxy forces, is a legitimate object for study by all ranks. The meaning of geopolitics, the importance of strategic minerals and the peril that could come from hostile control of key locations around the world concern all members of today's Armed Forces. Every commander can and should learn about those subjects. It is equally important to ensure that those in the command share that information. The Department of Defense and the various military schools have excellent materials that can be used for training and information programs. Many non-military texts are excellent, but care must be taken to avoid unreliable materials. Those based on heavy-handed scare charges or on recognized canards are dismissed as so much propaganda. The risk is that legitimate resource materials will be ignored or lumped with the street preacher's warning that the world is about to end.

The enormous costs of defense in modern times create opportunities for fraud or waste resulting in great costs to the government. Each officer has a duty and responsibility to keep constant watch to avert such costs, which not only have a monetary price but can affect morale and readiness. The officer in the junior ranks will seldom have an opportunity to affect "big picture" expenses, but the millions of smaller costs are under the control of the officer corps at all levels. They add up. As Sen. Everett Dirksen of Illinois said a generation ago, "A billion dollars here, a billion there, and the first thing you know you are dealing with real money!"

One generation ago, in terms of military personnel, the secretary of defense reported to the president that the largest defense budget the United States could afford in the foreseeable future was in the neighborhood of $15 billion. Within a year of that warning, the defense budget was doubled. Even that figure, which now sounds small, is a huge outlay of national resources. The entire defense budget is made up of individual items purchased, in most cases, from the lowest bidder. Each example of waste that defense critics can point to with alarm reduces the ability of the Defense Department to buy the essential equipment and supplies.

Each officer can ensure that equipment is used in the intended fashion, that supplies are not scattered aimlessly, that personnel are not assigned to useless tasks, and that critical funds are saved in many other ways. Being a guardian of the defense budget is the management part of a leader's responsibility.

Management also includes the responsibility to make sure that apparent economies do not come out of the pockets of service members. Curtailing on-base bus service may force some junior people to purchase automobiles. They may not be able to afford safe vehicles, insurance and upkeep.

Finally, in a review of current and future trends, it must be noted that the senior-subordinate relationship in the Armed Forces is more relaxed today than in some earlier generations. That does not mean that there has been, or should be, a relaxation of military courtesy and discipline.

High-technology equipment has produced a force of technicians, experts and skilled workers in uniform. Each is respected for individual skills and knowledge. Each still has a place in the chain of command, and each is obliged-by the organized teamwork required-to be both an effective leader and a conscientious follower. That is the essence of military professionalism. It produces mutual respect among officer and enlisted personnel. Where that respect exists, an effective organization is at work.

Suggested Reading

Biography and Memoirs:

General of the Army Douglas MacArthur, *Reminiscences*, McGraw-Hill, New York, 1964

General of the Army Dwight D. Eisenhower, *Crusade in Europe*, Doubleday, Garden City, 1948

Edgar Puryear Jr., *Nineteen Stars*, Coiner Publications, Washington, 1971

Captain Harry Butcher, USNR, *My Three Years With Eisenhower;* Simon and Schuster, New York, 1946nn

Secretary of Defense James Forrestal, Ed. by Walter Millis, *The Forrestal Diaries*, Viking Press, New York, 1951

General Lucius D. Clay, *Decision in Germany*, Doubleday, Garden City, 1950

Martin Blumenson, *Mark Clark*, Congdon & Weed, New York, 1984

Russell Weigley, *Eisenhower's Lieutenants*, Indiana University Press, Bloomington, 1981

General of the Air Force H.H. Arnold, *Global Mission*, Harper Bros. New York, 1949

General Curtis LeMay, with MacKinlay Kantor, *Mission With LeMay*, Doubleday, Garden City, 1965

Edgar Puryear Jr., *Stars in Flight*, Presidio Press, Novato, 1981

DeWitt S. Copp, *A Few Great Captains*, Doubleday, Garden City, 1980

Thomas M. Coffey, *Decision Over Schweinfurt*, David McCay, New York, 1977

Brig. Gen. Chuck Yeager and Leo Janor, *Yeager;* Bantam New York, 1985

James Parton, *Air Force Spoken Here*, Adler & Adler, Bethesda, 1986
Ordeals:

Colonel Robinson Risner, *The Passing of the Night*, Random House, New York, 1973

Vice Admiral James and Sybil Stockdale, *In Love and War* Harper & Row, New York, 1984

Strategy and Military Philosophy:

Brigadier General Dale O. Smith, *US. Military Doctrine*, Duell, Sloan & Pearce, New York, 1955

Major Thomas R. Phillips, Ed., *Roots of Strategy: Sun Tzu, Vegetius, de Saxe, Frederick the Great, and Napoleon*, Military Service Publ. Co., Harrisburg, 1940

Secretary of Defense Melvin R. Laird, *A House Divided*, Henry Regnery, Chicago, 1962

President Richard Nixon, *No More Vietnams*, Arbor Rouse, New York, 1985

General Bruce Palmer Jr., Ed., *Grand Strategy for the 1980s*, by Generals Bruce K. Holloway, Theodore Ross Milton, Bruce Palmer Jr., and Maxwell D. Taylor and Admiral Elmo R. Zumwalt Jr. American Enterprise Institute for Public Policy Research, Washington, 1978

General Bruce C. Clarke, *Guidelines for the Leader and Commander*, Stackpole, Harrisburg, 1963 ff.

James Barr and William E. *Howard, Polaris!*, Harcourt, Brace and Company, New York, 1960

Fleet Admiral William E Halsey and Lieutenant Commander I Bryan III, *Halsey's Story*, McGraw-Hill, New York, 1947 ff

Colonel Malham Wakin, Ed., *War, Morality and the Military Profession*, Westview Press, Boulder, 2nd Edition, 1986

Acknowledgments

This revision was prepared by Brian P. McMahon Sr. and John Causten
Currey, who offer the following acknowledgments: The advisory board,
which gave freely of time, knowledge and wisdom to direct the effort,
consisted of Lt. Gen. John F. Forrest, USA-Ret.; Lt. Gen. Albert P.
Clark, USAF-Ret.; Maj. Gen. Warren Moore, USAF-Ret.; Rear Adm.
Norman Coleman, USNR-Ret.; and Lt. Catherine J. Williamson, USN.
Their assistance and guidance were invaluable.

Special thanks go to Col. Malham Wakin, the permanent professor and
department head for philosophy and fine arts at the U.S. Air Force Academy, for his thoughtful assistance in the areas of ethics and morality.
Gen. Ira Eaker and Father Theodore Hesburgh, CSC, opened doors so
the work could begin. Vice Adm. William Ramsey, USN, Lt. Gen. Winfield "Skip" Scott, USAF, Brig. Gen. David W. Winn, USAF-Ret., Rear
Adm. J.A. Baldwin, USN, Brig. Gen. Jesse Gatlin, USAF-Ret., Col.
Phillip D. Weinert, USA-Ret., and a host of others held the doors open
so the work could be completed.

Even the minority who believed the original version was a classic and
should not be revised have helped the thinking process. They forced
re-evaluation and argument of what should be included, emphasized or
omitted to provide a text relevant to the officer of today and tomorrow.

The Secretary of Defense
Washington

February 1988

THE ARMED FORCES OFFICER (DoD GEN-36A)- *This official Department of Defense publication is for the use of personnel in the military services.*

www.ingramcontent.com/pod-product-compliance
Lightning Source LLC
Chambersburg PA
CBHW070756290526
45795CB00002B/570